DREAMING

A TRIBUTE TO SELENA QUINTANILLA PÉREZ

EDITED BY ODILIA GALVÁN RODRÍGUEZ

FlowerSong Press
McAllen, Texas 78501
Copyright © 2020 FlowerSong Press

ISBN: 978-1-7345617-7-7

Published by FlowerSong Press
in the United States of America.
www.flowersongpress.com

Set in Adobe Garamond Pro

Design by Carlos Galván aka Hawk Beatz
Typeset by Matthew Revert
www.matthewrevert.com

DEDICATION

This anthology is dedicated to the memory and magical artistic legacy of Selena Quintanilla and to all others whom she inspired to live their dreams.

This book is also dedicated to Carlos Galván aka Hawk Beatz, another powerful musician and artist who went home way too soon.

Rest in peace and power both of you.

ACKNOWLEDGMENTS

The Things to Fight Against was originally published in Switchgrass Review and later appeared in the poetry collection *Small Fires.* *"Selena: a study of recurrence/worry* was originally published in Crab Orchard Review, both poems are by author José Angel Araguz. *Anything for Selenas* by Ruben Reyes Jr. appears as prose in *Acentos Review* February, 2019.

CONTENTS

FORWARD

The *Bidi Bidi Bom Bom* that keeps us dreaming...

Today, Selena would be 49 years old. She was three years and one week older than me. I didn't know that until I researched the date of her death for this anthology. I was born on April 23, 1974 in Brownsville, Tejas, along the same coast as Selena's childhood homes in Lake Jackson and Corpus Christi. Unlike the Quintanillas, my family was from Matamoros, Tamaulipas, Mexico. I was the first born in the U.S. and a woman, nonetheless. Like Selena's father, mi papi constantly reminded me that I am Mexican American and would have to work ten times as hard to prove it to everyone throughout my life. While reflecting on Selena's legacy I have to remind myself that this isn't about me, this is about Selena Quintanilla-Pérez — La Reyna, the mislabeled "Tex-Mex Madonna," the Grammy winner and now, the 25-year-old icon who crossed borders, literally and musically. Selena is a role-model for little brown girls, pochxs, macho men, and diverse fans of all ages. And yet, I never considered myself a devotee.

The truth is, I was raised in the equally brown town of Santa Ana, California and didn't know of Selena until she died. In the fall of 1994, I moved back to Tejas after leaving when I was four years old. In 1978, my father, who repeatedly said he wanted a better life for us, packed his family of five in a beat-up old truck and drove to Califas. For the years to come, I had no idea what Tejano culture meant. It was the Spanish Texas music some of my tías danced to and what my abuelo played on his accordion. Prior to his passing in 1988, my father echoed many quotes that can be pulled from Edward James Olmos' role in the 1997 *Selena* movie. Those days, I never understood the fascination with her tunes or the fact that no one ever spoke about her conservative upbringing as a Jehovah Witness. Sure, I like cumbias like most Mexican Catholics do. I had to dance to them at countless Mexican weddings, quinceañeras and backyard asadas with my father. But I didn't know Selena's life until she was murdered on March 31st, 1995 and her birthday on April 16th, 1995 was declared "Selena Day" in Texas.

I have yet to own a Selena anything. In fact, when I do come across a Selena t-shirt, sticker, knockoff pin, reusable HEB bag, I give it away to the biggest fans I know. Now you're wondering why I'm even writing this. Another truth, I questioned editor Odilia Galvan Rodriquez if I deserved to contribute to the works that you're about to read. But here's what I realized when I took some time to reconsider the invitation. Even I — someone who has never replayed Selena in headphones like Eneida P. Alcalde depicts in the short story "Como La Flor" or visited her life-size bronze statue off the Gulf of Mexico — have a deep connection to what her name symbolizes. Like Selena Pineda writes in her poem "Mi Nombre," her tocaya has made a name for herself that is now defined on its own. Regardless of the timeless "Anything for Salinas" quote, memes and gifs passing through our screens in 2020, people around the world know exactly how to say her name. Interpreting Selena, also means acknowledging that many women and queer gente of all backgrounds have had to rise from misogyny, cultural expectations and beyond imposed gender roles in order to really embrace our dreams. Really embrace the idea that we can accomplish more than what our parents ever had a chance to imagine for themselves, *or for anyone like us*.

Dreaming brings together lyrical renditions, little boys dancing "the washing machine," prayers over velas, and odes to purple, sparkly hips swaying to cumbia beats. There's thirty-three works of poetry, prose, and fiction on these pages that provide such narratives: "For Selena" by Timothy Daily-Valdés, "One of Us: Selena Quintanilla-Pérez" by Nancy de la Zerda, "La Milagrosa Selena" by Rubén Degollado and plenty more pieces showing the world the impact she continues to make on the dance floor and across generations. This anthology also offers affectionate portrayals of fierce retellings, forbidden lovers, rhinestone studded bras, and heartbroken fans by contributors such as José Ángel Araguz, Beatriz A. Ceja, Magaly Garcia, and Aseneth Garza Scott. Of course, we also have some raw and poignant pieces capturing Selena's humble stardom rising above a patriarchal society and amor prohibido, yet unexpectedly dying at the hands of a woman over greed.

So, I leave you with this: these pages are brimming with devotions, stories and poetry that helped me understand the various identities found within *Selenidad* (a term coined in the scholarly publication by Dr. Deborah Paredez in 2009). I know you will also find something relevant on the page because Selena is more than her fame, fashion line and forthcoming Netflix series — she is the *Bidi Bidi Bom Bom* that keeps a lot of us dreaming, singing, dancing and staring at the moon knowing we can all reach for more.

— Sarah Rafael García, author
of SanTana's Fairy Tales & founder of LibroMobile.

The Things to Fight Against

for Selena

José Angel Araguz

Onstage, mouth brimming with the Spanish
parents teased her with, maybe she looked
down and saw the cowboy hats, the boots
   and belt buckles, the purses, curls,
and children, maybe she saw herself,

thought: Of all the things to fight against,
sound's not one of them – sound of applause,
sound of gritos, sound of sparked cuetes,
   sound of beer cans gasping open,
sound of busses turning in the dark,

groaning in dreams, sound of R's rolling,
sound of birdwing flutter, sound of wind
over open water, sound of flags
   unfurling, sound of flame flaring
up and out of a struck match, sound of

a voice, my own Spanish unsure, chopped,
shaky, sound of a bullet breaking
through the air, sound of a newspaper

splayed on the wind, the news floating,
punched with the grace of long hair – her hair

now a cold blade of bronze, her statue
along the sea wall, to see her is
to see the tide forever turning,
    pulled and pulling away, is to
think again of her killer, crying
in her car in a stand-off, gripping
the gun which would later be broken
to pieces and thrown into the same
    waters the statue looks over,
is to hear my aunt again call us

a city of crabs in a bucket,
each of us clambering to get out
has another behind them – their face
    similar, a face we've grown with
and understand – dragging them back down.

Selena: a study of recurrence/worry

José Angel Araguz

Somebody died and it's okay to be Mexican.
No, really, this is good. I was worried
nobody would understand what it means to come
from a city named after the recurring body

of a martyr. No, really, this is good.
I worried a whole generation of young women
from a city named for wounds and resurrection
would suffer themselves to be stilled and lost. Now

I worry a whole generation of friends close
their fists around empty beer cans and walk
out the door to become lost, distilled memories.
You would think no one would sing here

again. That with beer cans in their fists
mothers would tell stories about a ghost
appearing should you sing here in this city,
should you ever go onstage, a whole generation

of mothers telling stories where not a ghost
but a microphone vanishes directly below a spotlight

that burns anyone who walks onstage, different moon
in a different sky where it is always night.

See, a whole city vanishes below the spotlight
of my erratic memory. Corpus Christi, my imagination
paints you as an indifferent sky where night
after night we tell stories about who we were.

You are more than my erratic memory and imagination,
more than the name of a wounded, returned body.
When at night I tell stories about Selena,
I know that it is more complicated than

the name on a statue, more complicated than
somebody died, and it's okay to be Mexican.
I know life is more complicated than
anyone can understand or hope to become.

In Remembrance of Selena

Muskaan Ayesha

Dulcet and delicate melodies escape her lips.
The sky sat at her feet.
The stars didn't dare write her destiny or she was one of them.
She had returned home:
Amongst the scintillating constellations.
The angels ached to hear her exalted voice.
She was aesthetically prominent.
The fireflies danced within her hair and honey glazed her tongue.
Lavenders utter her poetic words in remembrance and the moon
can't help but confess his adoration for her;
"I could fall in love with you." he says and writes the story of her
eyes in the sunrise.
She is the sun that the moon bows for.
She is the sun that stands tall and vibrant.
She is the sun that ignites fires in the heart of sunflowers.
Oh, how glorious a woman of passion is.
She is the Tango the Fates emerge in to tie the world together.
She is deliriously aesthete canvass inked in poetry.

The Final White Rose

Vanessa Caraveo

No one knew nor expected this
The dire news that was announced
that evening in March 1995
Our Tejano queen
would no longer be among us
Words cannot explain how shocked and
broken-hearted many were.

The world cried
For an irreplaceable queen had passed on
Her warm and genuine smile would now
be but a beautiful memory
And that one-of-a-kind twinkle in her eyes
would remain in our hearts forever.

The epitome of an accomplished Latina
Setting the bar high and leaving an example
Of how far talent, dedication and
will-power can take you
You broke glass ceilings for many today.

You captivated us with your beautiful voice
Your perfect dance movements perfectly
coordinated to your unforgettable cumbias
Beautiful songs that were heard over and over
Still remembered today as Tejano classics by many.

Do you know how many lives you touched?
Young and old
Young girls dressing with your same style
Karaoke bars still filled with many
singing your greatest hits.

Rest assured you had a positive impact
In your short stay on this earth
It is not the time you had in this world
But how many lives you were able to touch
during that time that truly matters.

I will not say farewell as there can never be a goodbye
For a beautiful and unique soul such as yours.
I humbly give you my final white rose
with a small tear in the corner of my eye
And I assure you that my everlasting love and
respect for you will forever live on.

Pétalos Blancos

Vanessa Caraveo

Pétalos blancos
Inocente como tu esencia de niña
Y esa sonrisa carismática que te caracterizaba
Inolvidable igual que tú.

Igual que una rosa blanca eras única
Desprendías alegría en cualquier lugar que estabas
Representabas no solo la mujer tejana, sino la mujer latina
dignamente
Y orgullosamente un buen ejemplo para tantas mujeres, sin
duda.

Delicada flor con sentimientos puros
Siempre encontrabas el bien en todos los que te rodeaban
Incluso de personas que no lo merecían
Tristemente el precio de tu corazón bondadoso fue caro.

Pétalos blancos similares a las lágrimas que se derramaron
En mucho lugares al saber la notica
Que una hermosa reina
Había fallecido dejando un gran vacío en este mundo

No importa el tiempo que pase
Tu leyenda y esencia seguirá viva
Solo los grandes llegan a lograr eso
Y tú, mi "*Selenas*", sin duda lo eres.

Que siempre descanses en paz mi reina
Y que te sigan cuidando y protegiendo estos pétalos blancos
Delicados, hermosos, y únicos
Como la doncella tejana que vivirá en muchos corazones por
siempre.

Como La Flor

Eneida P. Alcalde

Fourteen-year-old Clara walked to school with Julieta, finding comfort in her twin's company. Julieta swayed to Biggie's beats, the Walkman's headphones covering her ears. Her ponytail bounced, the glossy brown curls reaching past her shoulders. Clara ran her hand over her head, feeling her short bob. She tucked the sides of her hair behind her ears, brushing her fingers on the silver stud earrings Mami gave her for her birthday—allegedly a gift from Papi. Impossible, Clara knew. Papi had been in jail for over a year for dealing drugs.

As they neared the corner of 8th and Cumberland streets, the walk signal turned red. Cars drove past, heading west toward Hershey and Harrisburg—larger cities whose steep rents and high taxes were out of reach for Mami's budget. Julieta took out the candy-yellow Walkman from her puffer jacket's pocket and pressed the stop button. She slid the headphones off her ears and peered at Clara from under her bangs with her big round hazel eyes—the same shape and shade as Clara's. Clara turned away, focusing on the Victorian building in the block ahead. Its mint-green turret jutted up into the morning greyness, reminding Clara of an old castle—weathered like many buildings in their hometown of Lebanon.

Julieta nudged Clara's arm with her elbow. "What's wrong?"

Clara shrugged. "Miss my hair."

"It'll grow back."

Clara hid her hands in her corduroy jacket's pockets. The wool-lining warmed her cold fingers. She stared down at her stonewashed jeans and chunky black boots, the almost brand new pair Mami bought at the second-hand store. She heard Julieta eject the cassette and glanced up. Julieta flipped it over and inserted it back into the Walkman.

"Eres bella no matter what," Julieta said, her fake-gold hoopearrings swinging with her words. "Way prettier than that pig-nosed Sally."

Clara's lips trembled. "It'll take forever to grow back."

Julieta held out the Walkman. "Want to listen to music?"

"Nah, it's your turn. I prefer listening to it after school."

Julieta stuffed the Walkman in her jacket. "Cheer up. No one messes with my twin."

Clara scrunched her eyebrows. "What do you mean?"

Julieta smirked. "Sally better watch her back."

The walk sign turned green. Julieta grabbed Clara's hand, pulling her. They passed cars whose motors hummed in the cold. When they reached the sidewalk, Clara wriggled her hand free from Julieta's grasp. She stood by the newspaper vending machine outside the Victorian building—a picture of President Clinton on the newspaper visible through the glass panel. Clara leaned against the vending machine, crossing her arms over her chest. Julieta adjusted the straps of her backpack as she eyed Clara.

"What's the deal? We're going to be late for school."

Clara shrugged. "Doesn't matter. All you want to do is beat up Sally."

"Bitch deserves what's coming." Julieta pointed her finger at Clara. "And you know it."

Clara shook her head. "It's not worth it. Like you said, my hair will grow back."

Julieta blinked hard. "What did your teacher do when you cried?"

Clara glared, not in the mood to rehash last week's glue-hair incident with Sally. She walked past Julieta. After taking a few steps, she felt Julieta pull on her backpack. Clara spun around, yanking the backpack away. Julieta stepped up to Clara, standing inches from her face.

"So?" Julieta said, her breath warm on Clara's skin. "What did your teacher do?"

Clara bit her lower lip, tasting cherry lip balm. "I told you. She pulled me and Sally aside.

Asked what happened."

Julieta tilted her head. "¿Y?"

"Sally said she didn't do it. Blamed me for spilling glue on myself."

Julieta pursed her lips. "And your pendeja teacher believed her not you."

Clara remembered the glue all over her locks. The strands stuck together in clumps. She

sighed. "You're going to get in trouble."

Julieta narrowed her eyes. "I don't care."

Mami will."

Julieta shrugged and slid the headset on her ears. She marched in the direction of their school. Clara followed, staying close behind. Fifteen minutes later, Clara and Julieta ascended the gentle-sloping sidewalk that led to their school along with other students, some talking and laughing, others alone and silent. A grassy field stretched out to their left. A red pick-up truck drove past on the right, blasting the Spice Girls' latest hit. Cigarette smoke floated out of the driver's open window from where strands of red hair fluttered in the wind. It was Sally—smoking illegally as usual. More cars drove past. Some driven by parents dropping off their kids. Others driven by juniors and seniors.

As Clara and Julieta neared the end of the sidewalk, they passed the school's tennis courts. Up ahead, a row of four pillars lined Cedar High School's wide facade. Clara and Julieta walked across the lawn toward the red-brick building, passing students in groups, catching up with their friends. As they walked up the front steps, Sally approached from the parking lot. She climbed the steps by the right pillar, the farthest from Clara and Julieta. There, she greeted some girlfriends, seniors who had been on the homecoming court. Julieta side-eyed Sally. Clara reached for the headset, jerking it off Julieta's ears.

Julieta pushed Clara's hand away. "What the hell?"
"Don't get into trouble."
Julieta scowled. "Sally messed with the wrong Puerto Rican."
Clara opened her mouth to respond, but the school bell rang.

Clara and Julieta entered the school's front lobby through double-doors and headed into the central corridor. Yellow lights dotted the high ceiling. Students stopped at their lockers, lining the hall's walls. Others entered their classrooms, the doors on both sides of the hall.

Halfway down the corridor, two football players walked across Clara and Julieta. They whispered to each other while sharing quick glances with Julieta. Clara elbowed Julieta's arm to catch her attention.

"Yeah?" Julieta said, looking at her.

"Don't flirt."

Julieta laughed. "Cálmate. Handsome one's the quarterback. He's in my algebra class."

"Isn't he in eleventh grade?"

Julieta huffed. "So?"

"You're a freshman."

"And?"

"He should be in an eleventh-grade class."

Julieta shook her head. "Man, you're a comemierda. Papi would not approve."

"If Papi gets out of jail, he can have a say." Clara turned away, avoiding Julieta's reaction. Her classroom was up ahead. She stopped at the door.

Julieta raised her eyebrows. "You're not going to your locker?"

"I'll drop off my jacket later." Clara grabbed Julieta's hand. It felt warm in her cold grasp. She squeezed it. "You got to leave Sally alone. It's not worth it."

Julieta frowned and lifted her chin, pulling her hand away. She walked down the corridor, disappearing amongst the other students. Clara pushed the door open and stepped inside her class. She squinted, adjusting to the fluorescent lights that illuminated the room's bone-white walls. Two students sat at their desks: one at the back of the class slouched over and the other toward the middle, a baseball cap hiding his face. Clara walked to her seat in the front row. She slid off her backpack and unbuttoned her jacket. She sat in her seat and faced Mr. Candelar, sitting behind his metal desk in front of her. Pen in hand, he leafed through a book. Clara liked the blue cardigan he wore over a white- collared shirt. He closed the book and glanced up. Clara blushed at his gaze, a piercing icy blue, striking against his black hair.

"Clara," he said in his baritone voice. "How are you this morning?"

"I'm good, Mr. Candelar."

"¿Y tu hermana?" he asked, having met Julieta in detention hall last month.

"Está bien," she said, feeling her cheeks flush. He spoke perfect Spanish.

Mr. Candelar grinned, his teeth straight and porcelain white. "¿Y tu Mami?"

Clara remembered Mami's reaction after meeting Mr. Candelar for parent-teacher conferences. Mami considered him muy guapo—a real-life Clark Kent who flew out of a

Superman movie into her daughter's class.

"Está bien," Clara said.

Mr. Candelar winked. "Dale mis saludos."

Clara nodded, knowing Mami would be thrilled to hear he had asked about her.

More students strolled in, talking loudly. Mr. Candelar went back to his book. Clara pulled out her journal from under her desk along with a pen. She flipped through the journal until finding a blank page. She drew stick figures of Mami and Julieta. She drew Papi then crossed him off—drawing an X over his mustached face.

When the final morning bell rang and all thirty desks were filled with freshman, Mr. Candelar stood in front of the blackboard. Clipboard in hand, he looked out at the class with a slight smile on his lips. The students stared back at him.

He glanced at the attendance sheet secured on the clipboard. "Clara Arce."

Clara raised her hand. "Here."

He smiled at her as he marked the sheet with his pen. She smiled back.

As he called the next student's name, Clara stared at the stick figure of herself she had drawn next to her mother and sister. She picked up her pen and wrote *como la flor* underneath.

The bell rang at the end of the school day. Clara exited Cedar High's front entrance with other students. She skipped down the steps and headed to the tennis courts where she always met Julieta afterschool. Reaching the courts, Clara turned to face the school. She leaned back on the court's chain-link fence.

Students walked or drove past Clara, all heading downhill into town. Clara plucked out the Selena cassette from her jacket's pocket. She inspected the album cover, running her thumb over the plastic case. The cover featured a portrait of the singer—red-lipped and beautiful like always. Mami bought Selena's albums after Selena was murdered, believing the Mexican-American singer had been a good role model for all Latinas, including her daughters. But Julieta hated Selena's music, calling it "pop shit." So, Clara happily kept the albums for herself and listened to one cassette every day on the walk home from school.

A sedan with a broken headlight stopped by Clara. The quarterback in Julieta's algebra class gawked from the passenger's seat. The other football player sat in the driver's seat. Clara looked to the school, hoping Julieta came out soon.

The passenger's side window lowered. The quarterback stuck out his head. "You're Julieta's sister, right?"

Clara glanced at him, getting a better look in the afternoon light. He was Ricky-Martin level hot, but dumb. "We're twins," she said. "So yeah, that makes us sisters."

The quarterback chuckled. He cocked his head, raising an eyebrow. "You need a ride?"

Clara swallowed, knowing Mami forbade her and Julieta from having contact with boys outside the realm of school. She clutched the cassette tighter. "I don't know you."

"I'm Rory Martinez."

Clara glared. "You don't know me."

He bit his lower lip and grinned. "I know you. You're Julieta's fine virgin sister."

Rory's buddy cackled, slapping the steering wheel with his hands.

Clara's stomach lurched. The cassette fell from her grip, smacking the sidewalk. She bent to pick it up, her hands jittery. She grabbed the cassette—the plastic case was broken down the middle in two pieces. As she straightened up, Rory chuckled with his friend. She folded up her jacket's collar to hide her burning cheeks.

Rory stopped laughing. He narrowed his eyes on her and smirked. "Damn, beauty. Didn't mean to make you hot and bothered. I'll be seeing you around the way."

He licked his lips and blew her a kiss. The car drove off.

Clara breathed out and leaned against the fence, lowering the collar back in place. She fitted the plastic case together over the cassette, wondering if Rory ever spoke to Julieta the way he spoke to her. She stuffed the cassette in her pocket, thinking of telling Mami about the encounter. But Mami would blame her, as she always did for boys' attention.

The school's front doors slammed open. Clara's eyes widened. Students streamed out, spilling onto the lawn. Clara sprinted to the mob, hearing the screams of a fight. Upon reaching the brawl, Clara surveyed the twenty-or-so students gathered in a circle, cheering. She did not see Julieta. She pushed her way past three students to the center. Her chest tightened: Julieta sat on Sally's stomach, straddling her with her knees on each side, holding fistfuls of Sally's red hair in her hands. Dark blood dripped from Sally's nose.

"No, please. No!" Sally said.

Julieta struck her across the cheek. "Puta! Don't ever touch my sister!"

Julieta yanked Sally's hair with both hands. Sally shrieked.

"Close your eyes and promise me puta."

Sally whimpered and closed her eyes.

Julieta pulled a glue bottle from her jacket's pocket. "Promise me."

"I, I promise."

Julieta opened the glue bottle and held it over Sally's face. A white glob fell on Sally's forehead and oozed down her hair. Julieta punched her stomach. Sally coughed up spit.

Mr. Candelar barreled through the crowd. He ran to Julieta and wrapped his arms around her waist, hauling her off Sally. Julieta dropped the bottle, splattering glue on the grass.

He glared at the students, his face pink. "Go home! Or you'll all be in detention!"

The students scattered. Clara stood in place.

Julieta thrashed in Mr. Candelar's arms. He forced her to lie on the lawn, holding her hands behind her back. He placed his knees on top of her legs, constricting her movement.

He stared around and noticed Clara. "Go home."

Clara's breaths quickened. "What will I tell Mami?"

Mr. Candelar shook his head. "Tell her Julieta's in trouble."

Clara remembered Mami's reaction last time Julieta got detention. Mami beat both girls with a leather belt. She beat Julieta for getting into trouble. She beat Clara for not tattling on her sister for playing hooky from school.

"Clara," Mr. Candelar said. "Do you want to stay?"
Clara swallowed. "Yes."

Julieta lay still. Mr. Candelar took his knees off her legs and helped her stand, holding her wrists behind her back. He glanced at Clara.

"Wait in my classroom while Julieta meets with Principal Gordy." He pointed at Sally. "Help her up and follow me."

Clara neared Sally, who moaned with her hands covering her eyes. Her cheeks were inflamed. Blood congealed around her nose. Glue dried in her hair.

Clara leaned down. "Sally?"

Sally stopped moaning. Clara grabbed Sally's hands, pulling them off her face. Sally squinted at Clara—her left eye blood-shot. Clara hauled her up. Sally stood on wobbly legs, wiping her nose with her sweatshirt's sleeves. She hobbled to the school, following Mr. Candelar and Julieta who were already heading up the steps. Clara walked next to Sally, close enough to catch her if she stumbled.

When they reached the school's entrance, Clara pulled the door open, letting Sally stagger inside. Mr. Candelar waited, holding Julieta's arms behind her back. Julieta kept her head lowered, staring at the floor.

"Sally follow us," Mr. Candelar said. "Clara, I'll meet you

in my classroom."

"Wait," Julieta said, her voice groggy. "I have Clara's Walkman."

Mr. Candelar frowned. He looked at Clara then back at Julieta. "Where is it?"

"Right pocket."

Mr. Candelar let go of Julieta's right hand. She pulled out the Walkman from her pocket.

"Here," she said, holding it out.

Clara approached. As she reached for the Walkman, Julieta met her stare, a pained expression marked her face—similar to how Papi looked at Clara the night the police took him away in handcuffs. Clara's eyes blurred. She breathed out and grabbed the Walkman. It felt heavy in her grasp. Mr. Candelar walked away with Julieta toward the principal's office. Sally followed, not saying a word.

Clara stuck her fist in her pocket. She felt the plastic case—the crack in the middle—and pulled it out. She inserted the cassette into the Walkman and slid the headphones over her ears. She pressed play.

Selena's sweet voice erupted. Clara mouthed the words to the song and swayed her hips to the cumbia rhythm as she made her way down the corridor. When she entered Mr. Candelar's classroom, she closed her eyes, shutting out the world around her. She spun in circles, singing aloud, flourishing with the music—feeling unstoppable like Selena, a flower like no other.

Corazón de Reina

Vanessa Caraveo

El brillo de tus ojos jamás olvidare
Y esa sonrisa carismática llena de bondad
Aún puedo escuchar tu risa encantadora
Siempre lista para hacer una broma con buen humor.

Un verdadero orgullo para todo los Tejanos
Dejando en alto este estado
Indiscutiblemente nuestra reina Tejana
Jamás habrá otra como tú.

La mayoría de los artistas son pretensiosos
Se les "suben los aires" como decimos,
Pero jamás a ti mi reina
Lo que te distinguía siempre era tu humildad.

De cualquier edad, joven o viejo
Siempre estabas dispuesta dar un saludo cordial
Y más que eso, tomarte una foto o dar un autógrafo
Sin duda, pudieran aprender muchos famosos de tu ejemplo.

Cruzaste fronteras con tu música e idiomas mostrando
            lo bello del biculturalismo

Yo sé que hubieras llegado aún más lejos
Si tu vida no se hubiera terminado a tan corta edad
Tenías todo el potencial y talento para hacerlo sin duda.

El que más cautiva de todos tus encantos
Es tu gran corazón
Noble, amoroso, gentil, bondadoso, humilde, *único*
Una verdadera reina en todo sentido de la palabra.
Nos enseñaste que no existe un *amor prohibido*
Y *como la flor*, tu belleza interior y exterior nos deleitaba
No me queda más, que quedarme
      con los hermosos recuerdos que dejaste
Y tener el consuelo que tu legacía como
      nuestra Reina Tejana seguirá por siempre.

Corpus Christi: "Amor Prohibido"

Robin Carstensen

You and I were all endorphin-rush
on a Tejano-stretched
barrier reef and tide luring us down.
Two young women, teaching our hands
how to reach across the Chevy's vinyl seat,
driving up César Chávez boulevard
where a brick building we were looking for
dared us inside "Miembros Solamente."
Selena's "Baila Esta Cumbia"
crested through the gaps in the black-
-stuccoed walls as we made our way past
two leather-clad dykes into a dark foyer
where a tattooed one looked me up
and down and took your crumpled dollars.
I spied the performer through beaded partition—
one motion of sequins on her makeshift stage—
beginning to lip-sync "Amor Prohibido."
We soaked in the myriad eyes
plunging into each other, and the glitter ball
flashing over the throng. You swept me around
the dance floor to a Mazz ranchero:

"No Quiero Volver." I could follow your lead
like leaves after wind. You were pleased,
until I pulled your body gently, taking
charge, and you tensed like liquid glass
in flame. We seized everything
dazzling from each other. You--an aficionada
of Selena's "Como La Flor" and the old
school Juan Gabriel and Rocío Dúrcal,
whom I fell in love with as hard
when I heard "Cosas de Enamorados"
and Selena's "Enamorada de Ti"
and listened to them otra vez y vez
en cuando, you teaching me every palabra
until I sang in my sleep. You were corazón
and tongue swelling down my throat
with Corona and limón, and devoted lover
through a one-year blizzard de mucho
cariño and machismo that ended
in Monterrey with a phone book-hurling,
water glass-throwing, fist-through-mirrors
rage in Hotel Fiesta's hallway when I wanted
everything my way and you were sick
of me being princess. You were a (wo)man-
of-war, tentacles glistening over the Gulf

of Mexico, having swept me to shore
while still clutching me "dreaming
of you," my whole body burning.

Selena

Beatriz A. Ceja

I first heard stars can die when I was 9 years old.
I thought that the famous would become infamous.
Unstoppable forces that no one can harm and
one day I would reach them.

Her body shaped like a coke bottle,
making it nice to have the big hips and round booty,
Have brown skin and still have the men hear you and
the women admire you.
Dancing cumbias like her feet were made of something
magical that no one would be able to replicate.
"Bidi Bidi Bom Bom"
Were the sounds of my child hood days.

Waking up to the smells of my mother
making the tortillas, and my father stirring the menudo.
Being raised on the border, I was neither more Mexican
nor more American, I was Tejana.

Born in 1986 the same year Selena Quintanilla Perez
was female vocalist of the year.
So my first lullaby was her music.

My first step went to the rhythm of her songs.

A female icon.
Who saw no borders.
Because the stage was her home.
Showing us that we can twist our hips
in ways that we never knew we could.
She made it impossible not to sing "Carcacha" song
Every time you would get into your friends old beat up vehicle.
Because we all had that friend with the old beat up vehicle.
And every Mexican woman prayed
they could look as good as her in a bustier

In our culture women were usually required
to take a step back and let the men have the control,
but she changed it all.
Finally making it ok for a Hispanic
female to take the lead.
And for years I told my mother that is who I wanted to be.
But how do you tell a little girl that her image
of the American dream is crushed?

At a very young age I learned about tragedy and nightmares.
But it never stopped me from chasing dreams.
Selena Quintanilla Perez

you are gone but you are not forgotten.

We will not give your murderer the fame
by questioning her motives behind your tragedy.
But reminding the world that you were the queen of Tejano.
The image to the Tex-Mex female movement.

We found red lipstick stains on her microphones and
not on those claiming to be her lovers.
So we know performing was her passion,
family was her life, and her *Amor Prohibido*
was the man she was married with until her last day of life.

And to a little chubby girl being told she would never
stand in front of a microphone, she meant everything.

I stand here.
I am a woman.
I am Mexican

I am American

I AM PROUD.
I am not afraid to have my voice be heard.
But it could have never been done without the dream

of this little girl looking up to her Tejana queen.
And the strength to be assured that True Legends never die.

Selena, when the whole world is sleeping,
I stay up,
and think of you.

One of Us: Selena Quintanilla-Pérez

Nancy de la Zerda

The day Selena was killed, March 31st, 1995, I'd stopped at a Circle K to get a snack, when a young woman strode in and called out, "They just shot Selena!" Everyone froze. The girl went on to answer questions. Something about a motel parking lot in Corpus, a ring, not sure Selena would make it, etc. Chills crawled through me. My hair stood on end. What strikes me when I recall that moment is how the bearer of such horrid news assumed everyone knew Selena. There were all kinds of people in that store. But whoever didn't know her, soon would. Though we lost what might've been, the world learned what a Tejana can be.

I'd heard Selena on the radio and seen her on television. She kept winning Tejana Artist of the year. No one could beat that voice. Her style. Her sales. A week after her death, I bought a VHS Selena concert tape at an Austin flea market. It's a production of *Estamos en Tejas*, a group who hosted Selena's concert of October 25, 1992 at Rosedale Park, in San Antonio. I've watched it a hundred times. I'd put it away and come back. The surreal nature of seeing this diva goddess with her phenomenal voice singing, dancing, joking with fans at Rosedale, a neighborhood park, in the middle of our vast westside barrio, still amazes when I watch. As does the wonder that is her joy and my pain, still fresh, every time.

Here, I reflect about Selena's impact on the world how she was the first performer of Tejano music to win a grammy; how her best hits album is at the top of the Latin iTunes charts today, 23 years after her death, I know she is so much more than her music. She's speaking to a whole new world, and she'll live forever:

One of us, whose dreams had no borders
singer/songwriter, fashion designer, business woman,
de un barrio de "Corpos." Our diva. Not from México.
Ni de Hollywood. O de Nueva York like before. A Tejana diva,
for all the world to share. An eternal light por medio de su
talento and the Shakespearean-type tragedy that took her from
us.

She is one of us. De familia. Dutiful daughter, hija dichosa,
A Tejana who speaks Spanish así, medio pocho como yo.
With that astounding voice, voz divina, so full, so heavenly a
gift that helped pull her family from poverty.
She's asked: "You started singing when you were nine, right?"
Selena bares perfect teeth in her wide-as-Texas trademark smile,
huerca hemosa, siempre cariñosa, dice: "Well, I was six and a
half when I started singing in my family's restaurant. But there
were hard times. The business closed and we turned to our
music to get by."

In Selena, we see that a veces you have to eat a lot of "sandwiches de baloney" before you can get a plato de puffies at Ray's or a brisket de Bill Miller's. But those year of gigging out at débuts, picnics and proms made Selena a consummate performer in the video I watch of her at age 20, forever poised and charming to her fans, though she loves to clown around. Husband Chris Pérez with a slight eye roll rolling smirks at A.B., her brother, who nods knowingly, both on guitar behind her, and sister Suzette, oblivious, ecstatic on the drums. Selena makes faces and crosses her eyes at the cameras. Her mirth is contagious. Everyone watches with smiling eyes. Adoring her. She is one of us. Sings to us about us.

Dances cumbia and twirls about, toda sexy siempre Selena.

Sings what little girls already know.

Como el corazón palpita Biri Biri Bom Bom when love walks by.

And how we pray to our carcachas, our jalopies, sometimes, Ay, no dejes te tambalear. Don't quit me now.

poco a poquito, get me where I need to go.

Selena sings about amores prohibidos de distintas sociedades, Pos, qué dirá la gente, about forbidden loves caught between social circles kept apart as if by barbed wire in this Lone Star State of ours.

And Selena may be the queen of cumbia, but for me, she's la reina de la ranchera when she belts out "Qué Creías," my fave.

She calls for a male volunteer from the crowd. Then she says, "What?"

to a catcall and with fun in her heart purrs, "I love you, too, pero no te chifles conmigo." Don't get too familiar, vato. As if to make clear:

I may be up here performing for you in my black sequined brassiere, but I'm not yours to abuse. She really means, "Pórtate bien, pendejo," but she says it nice. Siempre graciosa, Selena. Muy professional!

"Ladies, this is how you tell your man off, okay?"

She turns to the guy she's pulled onstage, her make believe boyfriend. Her prop.

He stands, todo shy, but totalmente enrapturado por la linda hechizera.

Huerca hermosa, Selena.

About lost love, she tells us to let it go. Yo sé perder. I know loss.

Sí, cómo me duele, it hurts like hell, but what did you think?

¿Tú, qué creías? She flicks the guy's lapel with pointed finger. That I'd take you back?

Well, you see, darlin', it ain't so simple. She shakes her head. You're not needed here now. You can go to La Chihuahua.

Así es que puedes irte. She flings out her arm, points away, like,

Bae; there's the door.

Selena is one of us. She welcomes us to her stage. Little girls of all ages, dour-faced viejitas, even slightly buzzed men. Her message resonates: We can be sexy, but command respect. We can have fun, but we're not yours to abuse. Not our loves, not our friends, not our bosses, not our neighbors down the street, nor the guy in the White House. Selena sings about us, and shows us so much more. Her music is still tops. Va a vivir para siempre Selena.

Her message is same as Mamá's: Dáte por respetar.

Same as #MeToo and Aretha. Give me R.E.S.P.E.C.T. Un poquito, siquiera.

I am here, but I'm not yours to abuse.

Y cuídate de las envidias, for godsakes!!!

For Selena

Timothy Daily-Valdés

Someone said *Selena* the other day
but meant *Selena Gomez*
and I wanted to teach the girl who said it
about real música, back-in-the-day música.
I didn't know how without a whole afternoon.

Someone said *Selena* the other day
but meant the J-Lo flick.
You can't be penned in celluloid fronteras.
You're the only one we'd do anything for,
Nuestra Señora Como La Flor.

You taught me duende before I knew the word.
I could listen to your canciones all day, chingona.
You taught me what my childself could learn
of Tejanidad, Latinidad, Chicanismo
when no one else would. Que Dios te bendiga.

I tried to dance like you when
the girls on the playground would try to dance like you
porque you were la Reina
de Tejas de verdad and you knew

so much I didn't.

You knew how to fall in love, knew
the corazón's botany, knew me in a way
I didn't know myself yet. You were my first
patron saint. Santa Selena, show me the path
to fearless. I was six years old when a lady
who said she was your friend
tried to kill you. I cried
for a while como la Llorona

but I'd forgotten
that a person can't kill what isn't mortal,
can't touch an estrella.
They told me you were gone,
but you and I, hermana,
sabemos.

La Milagrosa Selena
Rubén Degollado

June 27, 1997

Dear Reymundo Peña, the Archbishop of the Diocese of Brownsville,

Even though I know La Milagrosa Selena Quintanilla Pérez the Queen of Tejano Music was a Jehovah's Witness, and was not baptized into the faith, I still believe she is a saint. Let me explain why.

First of all, I believe she should be canonized a saint regardless of not being baptized. Before I go any further, you have to know that I am more Catholic than a rebozo, more Catholic than the smell of incense, more Catholic than *persignando* when you drive by even the smallest Catholic church. I make the sign of the cross even when I see a sign pointing to a Church. So you have to know where I am coming from.

Even though the beautiful Selena Quintanilla Pérez is now gone (que descance en paz), murdered by that evil desgraciada Yolanda Saldívar (maldito sea su nombre), she healed my comadre Marisol Buentello. I know one of the things someone has to do to become a saint is to perform at least two miracles. Selena has already performed two, and I'll bet if I or anyone else looked for some more we would find out she did a lot more than this.

Healing my comadre was not the first thing she did.

Here are the known miracles Selena performed:

The First Known Miracle of Selena

The first thing she did in my comadre's life happened a year before Selena went to Heaven. My comadre got to see Selena with her own two eyes. Like the rest of us we had seen her on Puro Tejano. Even though comadre Marisol wasn't like that desgraciada Yolanda Saldívar, all in love with Selena, she still had a connection with her. Like the rest of us, she felt like she was family with Selena and was not all 'Soy tu fan!' about it. Watching her on the TV, trying to ignore Puro Tejano's host Rock-n-Roll James as he interrupted Selena's performances with his bad dancing and man-*chongo* was not like seeing Selena for real, up close and in all of her regal Tejana glory. It was in this moment, in seeing Selena for herself, that my comadre experienced the miracle of *La Milagrosa Selena*.

How *The First Known Miracle of Selena* came about was, a few years ago. Selena y Los Dinos went to play at the Villareal in McAllen and Lalo, my comadre's husband, bought them both tickets at the Boot Jack.

There was lots of people dancing and waving their hands. Comadre Marisol watched as all those people, the men in their silk shirts and gambler hats, the women with their tight jeans and high hairsprayed hair, danced in pure happiness. Comadre saw how they mouthed the words to all the songs. Selena shimmered in her green one-piece outfit showing her flat stomach, and she was twirling up on the stage, making those washing machine moves like she knew how to do. All the men couldn't take their eyes off her. The women couldn't stop looking at her either. Selena was that kind of person.

Comadre Marisol's favorite song "Como La Flor" came on and Lalo took them up front. He threw his shoulders into the crowd and they had to move for him. Eulalio Buentello is a big, wide man, about six feet tall with a thick beard, like a Mexican Grizzly Adams. Comadre Marisol just followed behind her husband. They finally got up there, and that was when it happened. I've known comadre Marisol for many years. There have only been a few times in her life when she says she felt a life-changing moment.

She got up to the front, and just for a second, Selena looked at my comadre. No big deal, right? Well, let me tell you, it was. Selena didn't just look at her like she looked at all her fans.

Selena looked down from the stage into comadre Marisol's face. She looked like someone does when they think they know you, but they're not sure.

Comadre Marisol smiled. Even though she was older than Selena by about ten years, had three children and had lived life more, she felt like a chiquilla again. Comadre Marisol felt like an angel was smiling at her.

Then, Selena performed *the first known miracle*. She held out her hand to comadre Marisol and made the OK sign with her fingers. She mouthed the words, "Everything's going to be okay," just as comadre Marisol was thinking them in her mind. Selena must have had a *dón espiritual* to see inside my comadre's heart. You see, comadre Marisol always says this to herself when she's scared or sad. She looks into the mirror, makes the sign with her hands and says, "Everything's going to be okay," just like her father used to do before he got sick. But that is a whole other story, for someone else to tell. I could go off and tell you about her whole sad life and family history, but for the purpose of why I am writing you today it is not important. What was important and astonishing was that as all those hundreds and thousands of fans were saying the words to Selena's songs, Selena was singing the words to the song of comadre Marisol's life. You can't get more amazing than that.

The Second Known Miracle of Selena

This miracle I know about is what caused me to think about the miracles Selena has performed. This is what got me to write to you.

Selena healed my comadre Marisol of her sickness. My comadre didn't have cancer or AIDS or anything serious like that. Yes, she has susto, always afraid that something bad is going to happen to her kids. But that isn't her biggest problem; it's her eating. No, she's not one of those women who starve themselves into skeletons. She knows how sick those pobrecitas look.

Here was her eating problem. Almost every night for about a month, when Lalo and the kids were sleeping, comadre Marisol would get up out of bed and go to the refrigerator. She would sleepwalk and eat cookies, pan dulce, leftovers from Molina's barbacoa, El Pato, La Casa Del Taco, China Palace,

Red Barn barbecue, Casa Don Eusebio botana platter. She'd also eat peanut butter and jelly, cereal, etc. She ate so many other things while she was asleep, I can't even imagine. Comadre Marisol says she never remembered getting up, and she couldn't stop herself. The difference with her and one of those bulimics was one, she was sleepwalking when she did it and two, she didn't throw up. She just kept it all inside of her, and then she went back to her bed that way with a big full panza. Since it had started, almost a year before, she had gained almost sixty pounds. Like I said, she is beautiful. I think so and Lalo thinks so. But, I was really afraid for her health. She didn't want to explain to Lalo how the food was disappearing and how nothing was put away in the morning. The thing was, she didn't want him to think she was going crazy like other people in her family have gone crazy. Again, I don't want to say too much about her family because it isn't for me to share. She couldn't hide what was happening though. One morning, after a night of having fed her face like that, she called me up and said she needed me to come over.

When I went over to her house, she said, "Ay comadre, I just don't want to live this way." What could I tell her? I didn't know what to say.

My comadre and me were not alone. Another woman was

with her, comadre Marisol's sister-in-law, Victoria, who is married to Marisol's oldest brother. I don't feel comfortable telling you her last name. She was wearing nurse's clothes. I had seen her once or twice at comadre Marisol's mother's house. Automatically, I knew why she was there. I had heard that Victoria prayed for people and they got better. She was like a curandera without all the powders and hierbas. Supposedly, the only power she used was the Holy Spirit and anointing oil. The thing was, she was from one of those man-made churches that broke away from the One True Church. I sucked my teeth when I saw her and couldn't help myself from wrinkling up my nose and making my face all pinched. Obviously, comadre Marisol must not have thought I was enough to help her.

Victoria was listening to comadre Marisol go on about how she hated herself for the things she was doing, living that lie that everything was okay with her.

"Ay, I just don't know about this terrible life." She looked so old and sad, Padre, like all the good things in her life had never happened. Victoria didn't know what to say because I don't think she'd ever dealt with something like this. Victoria looked like one of the flacas who had everything she wanted. I didn't understand why she had invited her. She couldn't even come close to understanding comadre Marisol's situation.

Then I broke in and said, "You have so much, a husband who loves you, works for you, and three kids who don't get into too much trouble. Your girls are beautiful just like you."

Comadre Marisol nodded and said, "Pues si, pues si, you're right about that."

Victoria started talking, saying that if comadre really wanted to be healed she had to have faith and the Spirit of God living inside of her.

Comadre Marisol said, "Whatever it takes."

Then they prayed what Victoria called the sinner's prayer, where she and comadre Marisol asked God to take away her sins and to baptize her with the Holy Spirit (even though we both know that was done during Baptism and she was baptized with the Holy Spirit upon Confirmation).

Comadre Marisol's whole body was shaking with crying as Victoria had her hands on her head, anointing her, saying, "She has confessed to you, heal her Father, heal her. Sanela, sanela, en el nombre de Jesus we rebuke this sickness, we speak against it."

When they were done and comadre Marisol calmed down, I just sat there watching, wondering why she had even invited me if all I was going to do was watch them pray and hug and cry.

Then, like Selena had given me a message from heaven (yes, Selena is in heaven and God has looked past her JW past), I knew exactly what to do.

I got up and went to her stereo and turned on the CD player.

Of course Selena was in there, so "Techno Cumbia" was what I put on. It took comadre Marisol a little while, but soon, after me asking her to get up off of the couch and join me, we were swinging our hips, doing the Selena twist like we know how.

Victoria just sat on the couch not sure what to do for a couple of seconds, but then she too got up, and went against her religion. She was now on the carpet with us, all of us swiveling and twisting comadre Marisol's sadness away. I saw all those tears drying on comadre Marisol's face, and I knew Selena was healing her from the grave. All that sickness of eating herself to death was leaving her body like an evil night air burning away with the sun. The mal viento that had passed over her life was now gone.

The miracle did not end with us dancing in comadre Marisol's living room, I bought her one of those CD walkmen so she could fall asleep with Selena's songs. Every night after that, comadre Marisol put her headphones on. Selena's music came to her as she fell asleep, as if through the cosmos all the way from heaven, and she never got up in the middle of the night to eat all that food. She didn't need to do that because *La Milagrosa Selena's* music filled the emptiness inside of her. Every night now, Selena visits comadre Marisol in that magic place between dreams and being awake and sings, "Everything's going to be okay." Selena does this and comadre Marisol knows that all her problems are so small compared to the love of Selena's heart, to the everlasting reach of Selena's songs.

My comadre Marisol is even more beautiful now that she is losing a little weight. It's not the weight, really. It's what she thinks about herself that is changing her whole face, making her even prettier than she was when she was a teenager. Lalo is the only one who doesn't seem to notice how much prettier she is becoming. To him she is the same gorgeous woman she always was.

So, you see Padre Peña, *La Milagrosa Selena* (that will be her new name) performed a miracle on my comadre Marisol and continues to do so every night. She took a woman who was trapped in sadness and freed her. I know it is a miracle since *La Milagrosa Selena* spoke to both comadre Marisol and me. And I myself saw my comadre healed. I hope you believe in *The Three Known Miracles of Selena*, and do everything you can to make sure *La Milagrosa Selena* becomes a saint.

If you do not believe me, or think Selena is outside of grace, don't worry because God will forgive your blindness to the truth of what comadre Marisol, Victoria and I witnessed. He is good that way, to forgive us no matter what. If you do believe, but do not help me in my efforts to make *La Milagrosa Selena* an official saint because you are afraid of what people will think, I will not hold it against you. You have to do what you have to do. However, un aviso, I tell you this. When people hear of this miracle, and you don't recognize it as a miracle, they will still believe. For miles and miles, they will hear this story and *La Milagrosa Selena* and her music will heal them too. At yerberías and tiendas botánicas, and grocery stores all over the Valley, and wherever there are Mexicans, Selena's candles will be next to Jesus and Mary's, the Five African Powers and El Niño Fidencio Constantino's. All you will be able to do is ignore what is happening.

Whatever you decide to do, gracias for listening. God bless.

Sincerely,

Lourdes Montelongo Sepúlveda

The Night I Saw Selena at PBD's in McAllen, Texas

César L. de León

but it couldn't have been
i'd seen Her statue in corpus christi
seen the bouquets of yellow
roses tied with purple satin ribbons
gathered at her feet
caressed by the gulf coast breeze
the south texas sun
the seagull song
yet there She was
      La Reina
      gliding over the checkered dancefloor
            disco lights swimming around her boots
                hips swaying above purple bell-bottoms

      side to side
            side to side
                    side   to   side

      to the center of the room

            frozen
inhaling deep   holding

                        contando
            ¡uno!
                        cheers arched
                                    across the room and up
                                    back from 1995
¡dos!
back from houston
 back from the astrodome
¡tres!
                    "how you doing, houston texas!"
                                    Her voice
 angelic through dusty speakers
            made the young man next to me wipe tears from his
eyes
            made couples forget their drinks at the bar and flank
the pista
            and from their glittery corner made drag queens scream
out
                                    "i love you Selena!"
purple sequin disco-cumbia-hips
            bumped against the spotlight that followed
                                    long black hair
red chicana lips
                    twirls
                    clapping hands

booty and legs for days driving the beat
and all the jotería sang
and all the jotería danced
even the "straight-acting" cowboys
                    like the one in black hat
who took me in his rough hands
                    and spun me around three times
                    while She smiled from afar
at me
at the crowd
          and we could almost touch her
          almost
and we were blessed

Roses in My Throat

Magaly Garcia

On a recent night of green apple flavored Four Loko, my being lightweight resulted in me oversharing with my sister several personal shames of mine.

Most of what I revealed that night was not new to my sister. She had long since been familiar with my reluctance to step back into the public education field as a career option. What was new to her that night were certain details behind my disillusion of teacher-hood, birthed from a single reaction of mine in the third grade.

My first love was Shakira.

Her wiggly belly, vibrating vocals, and entrancing songs inspired me to shake my legs and toss my hair left and right. Growing up, I sang and danced to her English and Spanish songs, along with other hits like Selena's "Bidi Bidi Bom Bom" and "La Bomba" by Azul Azul.

But in the third grade, during a single-file walk back to class after lunch and recess, my best friend and I complimented each other's singing. When she told me I sang better in Spanish than I did in English, though, I was outraged.

Since my earliest memory, I was constantly reminded by my parents, teachers, and classmates of the fact I live in the United States. It did not matter that we lived in el Rio Grande Valle. It did not matter that we lived half an hour away from the International Bridge. It did not matter that beloved relatives resided in México and only communicated in Spanish—according to everyone, from men in suits to cashiers in carnicerías, speaking English equalized success for immigrant parents and their children.

As a result of the English-only glorification, my mother required me to read and write in that one language the moment I reached the age of four, slapping rulers on my knuckles each time I miscopied kindergarten level English terms. By the time I reached the third grade, I internalized the idea that my English had to be perfect, mainly because if I got a 99 on a spelling quiz, my mother would forbid me from watching cartoons on Canal 5.

This aim for flawless English was reinforced by my teachers as well, whose goal was to help students transcend from English as a Second Language lessons to higher curriculum classes which were solely lectured in English. It was no secret that to move up the ranks of successful students and to pass state exams, one must stick to English. In the process of embracing this knowledge, I and several others learned to disapprove of and drop most of our Spanish. By the middle of my third grade year, I was transferred to an all-English class located at the entrance of the third-grade hallway, way at the opposite end from where my bilingual class stood.

No Spanish, those English-only teachers would say with a tap of their heels and crossed arms. No Spanish books. No talking to each other in Spanish. No homework assignments can be turned in if they are completed in Spanish. I do not want to hear a single Spanish word in this classroom, understand?

Like the obedient children we were, we nodded along in acceptance of the rule, further internalizing the belief that everything sounded better in the language our parents wanted us to learn even though they did not speak it.

Still, I continued singing and dancing to Spanish at home as if nothing happened. At the time, in my child mind, nothing did.

Then, in the fifth grade, I got sick.

In that school year, my teacher was a woman who interrupted my reading-aloud each time I mispronounced words. Specifically, words that contained the side-by-side combination of two letters: t and h.

"The," "this," "that"—I never realized until this teacher made me repeat myself in front of the rest of the students that I was saying, "de," "dis," "dat." Apparently, neither English cartoons, strict single parenting, (my parents divorced the previous year) or English-only teaching, prepared me for the realization that I had not been using my lips, tongue, and teeth correctly for a specific sound commonly used in English.

To make matters worse, it was no secret this teacher disliked me—I was a narcissistic kid frustrated over my parents' divorce. Knowing she found something to shame me with was mortifying, so getting sick and not attending school for a day was a pleasant change of environment.

On that sick day of mine, my mother took me with her to work.

Throughout those first few years after her divorce, my mother mostly found employment cleaning houses. At the time, she worked for a mother of two toddlers who I would play or watch movies with, and the movie I sat through with them on that day was Selena.

In the beginning, I was disinterested, preferring animated films over live-action dramas. I paid attention anyway, and quickly found myself charmed by the scene when Selena's father taught her how to roll her r's to improve her Spanish pronunciation.

On that day, my love for Selena was born. On that same day, I experienced heartbreak upon discovering she was no longer with us, and a little seed of something I did not know what to call at the time got wedged somewhere in my throat.

See, I grew up with Selena's music just as much as I grew up listening to Shakira. I loved her wardrobe and voice, and I danced and sang along to her unforgettable tunes for as long as I could remember. For some reason, though, I never paid attention to the artist of "Amor Prohibido" or "Como la Flor" until I discovered I lost her.

Unfortunately, my newfound love for the late Tejana artist was still not enough to convince me to better appreciate Spanish until I reached the 8th grade, when I learned about a contradiction of demands for students in high school and college:

To graduate, we needed to obtain a required amount of credits in a foreign language. And in el Rio Grande Valle, the only language offered in most public schools, including mine, was Spanish.

I entered an Advanced Placement Spanish class out of pure luck and struggled for the entire year. No matter how hard I listened, I couldn't hear where accents went in Spanish spelling. No matter how much I practiced my speech, I couldn't pinpoint the appropriate times to use "mujer," "señora," or "señorita" in Spanish sentences. No matter how high my grades were at the end of the year, I walked out of the classroom confused by how little I reconnected with the language I once was fluent in.

Without the presence of my parents' home language in the classroom, most of my español dissipated from my vocabulary before I reached middle school, as was the case for many students in the district. Most of my unilingual companions and classmates either lost their linguistic skills or never developed them, therefore rejecting the language by the time we were told we needed it.

Why do I need to learn Spanish now? I never had to before, and Oh my god—that's embarrassing. Those idiots should stop playing that. We're not in Mexico, were common statements made by such students whenever *corridos* were played during the half hour lunch break in high school, when accordion notes echoed across the parking lot from the chain-link fence to the school patio.

Many teachers shared this same sentiment; during a code-switching conversation between my friends and I, all of whom either outgrew the English-only elitism or never bought that mentality, our AP World History teacher turned to us and said:

I don't understand why you have to butcher both languages. It sounds awful. This is why they tell you to only stick to one language. I never taught my kids Spanish and I don't understand the big deal everyone makes out of it. They are not going to use it or need it in their lives, not even for their careers.

This shushing of Spanish and Tex-Mex mouths began leaving a bad taste on my tongue, and the seed planted in my throat since my fifth grade sick day grew a rosebud of something I still could not name.

Despite these voice-silencing observations, I still did not fully submerge myself in my first language until I reached my junior year of undergrad schooling, when a professor recommended I include some Spanish in my writing. That was the second time I incorporated the language in an assignment, aside from that one year of AP Spanish. Since then, that rosebud of something opened, and I tasted my love for Tex-Mex, Spanglish, and the Spanish I am now struggling to recover.

Because of my long-awaited reunion with my first language, I forgot how Texas public education dealt with native tongues. My reminder was a single year of working as a tutor in a public school.

I arrived at the middle school eager to wake up early and tutor students on how to improve their writing and grammar skills so they could better prepare themselves for high school and college. Months into my work in that middle school, I witnessed an AP English teacher snapping at her students when a couple of them were chattering in Spanish.

We're not in Mexico—speak English!

In that instant, I was that student looking back at the teacher with shame in her eyes.

In that instant, I was the surrounding students smugly agreeing with said teacher.

When the end of the year came around, I lied when I was

asked if I was willing to return the following school year. And several years later, all of this was wailed out to my sister, who probably held my hand as she continued to finish her own can of Four Loko. I don't know. I no longer remember.

But one thing I did not tell my sister on that night was that I have been my own personal educator: I have been reteaching myself how to sing in Spanish for the past few years, from the sitting-straight-up vowels to the stern pronunciation of certain words, unlike those in English with "th."

The first singer I belted out my voice to again, albeit unsuccessfully, was Shakira, with her recent flirtatious hits and hypnotizing hips.

Now, when the taste of roses rises in my throat, I honor Selena's vocals and love for the Spanish tongue.

My Selena

Aseneth Garza Scott

Selena –

The first movie I ever stayed awake for that my father and step-mother took me to.

When it ended, I clapped joyfully for making it through.
I did not assimilate then the loss of someone that could represent me and my culture on screen.

About a year after her death, I got to see her again through an impersonator.
I even have a picture of her when she visited us in Port Isabel, Texas.
She wore a beautiful bustier, and I thought, Selena's dad would be upset.

At Head Start we got to do yearly performances.
She was my go-to artist.
I loved practicing those washer machine cumbia moves as I imagined myself a young Selena along the Corpus Christi shores.

In college, I took a class on identity, and that Edward James Olmos phrase came up:

> "We have to be more Mexican than the Mexicans and more American than the Americans, both at the same time! It's exhausting!"

My world started to make sense and once again, Selena was there to guide me.

As a member of Chicano caucus, we held a movie screening.
We introduced Selena the person and Selena the movie at Princeton.
It was a room full of Ivy Leaguers who had no clue who she was.
We celebrated the acknowledgement of our cultures and the worlds we shared with pizza and hot sauce.

Nostalgia

Por Aseneth Garza Scott

Solo fotos y recuerdos
Me quedan de esa etapa

Cuando aprendía el inglés
y mejoraba mi español

Quería ser parte de esos dos mundos
      El Americano y Mexicano
        Compitiendo a ser mejor en ambos

Pero lo único que me salía bien era
bailar al ritmo de la *Tecnocumbia*

Enamorada de ti

Erika Elisa Garza

Sé que eres un
amor prohibido
que
no me queda más
que olvidarme de ti
y continuar
dreaming of you
cantándote sin que me escuches…

Tú solo tú
con la música me enamoraste,
fotos y recuerdos
de lo que pudo ser y no fue,
como la flor
que nunca me diste,
la llamada
que nunca escuché.

No sé quién fue más
cobarde.
Si tú por alejarte o yo por no luchar.
Pero sé que no debemos ser ni

buenos amigos
ni amantes, ni antes, ni ahora, ni nunca,
no debo y
no debes jugar.
Pero
ya ves
aunque me pagaste con
tus desprecios
mi corazón canta
bidi bidi bom bom
y salta cada vez que te ve a lo lejos
wondering si me extrañas, si me sueñas.

Si una vez
recuerdas how you and
I could fall in love,
We, bailando *forever* abrazados
hasta la última canción,
escondiendo mi amor
esperaré el especial encuentro extrañándote eternamente...

A White Guy Hearing Selena's "Siempre Hace Frio" for the First Time

Michael Gerleman

Two souls, one car, on a dark South Texas night.
        We ride in silence, my eyes on the road,
        her face bathed in her iPhone's soft, blue light.
"Why don't you speak Spanish?" while still looking at her
phone.
        How could I explain that my clumsy tongue,
shattered the Spanish against the walls of my mouth,
and turned a babbling brook of a language,
into a dark muddy puddle?
How could I explain the words batted like butterflies
against my ears, refusing to land?
"Hey, listen to this!" A tap on the screen
        and a voice filled the car.
      If voices had color, this voice would be a
dark amber. If voices had shapes, this voice would
        look like a dark, wild honeycomb.
It was full of the emptiness of anguish and loss.
 I understood every word, even though I didn't
know any word. The voice told me all. Someone
was gone, someone was lonely, someone was sad.
The voice transcended the language of men. I needed

no translator, no guidebook to navigate this land.
It was all clear.
The singer was teaching me a new language-
the language of love and loss.

Pero sé que no debemos ser ni

"I Know How To Lose"

Monique Hayes

When their family's first greenhouse burned down, her older sister Terry never forgave Arianna Isabella Reyes for rushing into the inferno to rescue her mother's BeDazzler. Such a novelty from the local Luz Crafts store wasn't worth the risk. Once outside, Arianna examined the charred edges of the tool while a plume of smoke swirled over the smoldering perennials. She tried to envision rhinestone-studded outfits instead of ruined freesias but she couldn't ignore the ruthlessness of the flames behind her ten-year old back.

Not doing any glittery ornamentation helped dull Arianna's memory of Terry yelling at her while the doctors checked her lungs. Arianna chose to love jeweled jeans from afar once they relocated to Lake Jackson. City bus passengers bounded into their seats with spangled names on their pants legs. Drops of Krazy Glue surrounded the faux diamonds attached to their pockets. Arianna closed her eyes to shut out the sea of colorful stones even though she wanted to drown in them every time.

There proved to be one day when she couldn't look away thanks to three Tejano princesses. They weren't truly royalty but Arianna admired the girls' carriage as they waltzed by her with their ice-blue Discmans, beaded flower handbags, and bold ebony up-dos.

Their machines played the same muffled song but Arianna knew the lyrics perfectly. How could she forget huddling with Terry under her comforter a year ago as they both sang "Como La Flor"? They imagined they were under the lights of the Houston Astrodome, garden soil still caked to their shoes, gesticulating with their arms on the mattress like it was a grand stage. Arianna cared more about imitating her favorite belter back then than in fashioning flawless belts.

Arianna approached her fellow passengers with shaky steps as the bus reached its next destination. The girls gave her a suspicious look when she handed them twenty dollars.

"Could I buy one of your Selena CDs?" asked Arianna.

"Sorry, but we need them," replied the most petite princess. "We're memorizing Como La Flor for our school variety show."

"Okay," said Arianna.

She wouldn't have given up the disc either if she were in their shoes. It was a foolish hope but Arianna hoped it might help Terry's hopelessness. After the second greenhouse was firmly planted in Lake Jackson, Arianna thought there would be a flicker of the old Terry again. The old Terry didn't mind being called Teresa Fresca since she was addicted to the soft drink. She climbed trees to eat crispy chalupas and humored Arianna when her little sister swore her Bubble Beeper gum was an authentic beeper. Unfortunately, the old Terry had yet to make another appearance and her replacement seldom smiled or laughed. She did work but nobody, including their beleaguered father, wanted Terry to stay behind glass walls forever. At least the CD would've reminded Terry of their makeshift concerts under the covers and maybe inspire her to grin more.

"We really want to nail it!" chimed in the tallest princess.

"Well," said Arianna, recalling the way old Terry used her ruler as a microphone. "Do you need help with your costumes?"

The two Reyes sisters were infamous for doing cartwheel races down the first greenhouse's rows when Arianna was smaller than some of the shrubs. With their parents tending to various types of flora after hours with the watering cans, Arianna and Terry's limbs would flip sideways in the twilight hours. Lean and quick Terry usually won. Arianna remained stout, with minor growth spurts, a trait she shared with her mother Rosalita. Rosalita was also a master seamstress who repaired their clothes whenever their energetic excursions ripped them apart.

Arianna failed to sprint or contort her body when she returned to the greenhouse after the bus ride. She shoved her hands, full of indentations from lovingly grasping gemstones, into her shorts. Terry stood in the center of the structure doing Arianna's single chore for the day. Arianna had forgotten that the bulbs had to be unpacked before the next delivery arrived. She lost all those races and she was on the verge of losing her family's respect, which was more important to her than any win.

"I'll do it!" insisted Arianna, rushing to Terry's side.

"Where were you?" groaned Terry. "I swear if you were doodling dresses in that book again…"

Terry wouldn't understand if Arianna told her about the magical bus ride. The princesses were kind in letting her sort through their old spangled costumes. She thought holding the tulle was the closest she'd ever come to touching a cloud. The scarlet silk tops were the brassiest shirts she'd ever seen. Carmelita, Patricia, and Inez agreed that a fourth hand was just what they needed. Arianna reassured them she had tons of experience with sewing and stud setting. As far as she was concerned, her sketchbook would seal the deal.

"I'm not doodling!" cried Arianna. "I'm designing...for real people! These girls want ideas for their new skirts."

Flecks of dirt fell to Terry's forehead as she took her bandana off. Arianna squinted at the unexciting turquoise fabric under the greenhouse's bright lavender lamps.

"I've got some ideas for that, too," said Arianna.

Terry gripped the bandana tightly. "This is for work."

"That's going to be my work, Teresa Fresca," said Arianna. "All the stars will be wearing everything I create."

"I don't know many Lake Jackson girls who make it that far," whispered Terry.

Though the tulips wouldn't blossom for several weeks, Arianna believed Terry was considering another timeline in her mind. That timeline would've sent Terry to teacher's college a year ago, Arianna to the same private school Terry attended, and their parents on a second honeymoon to Tijuana. A lot of dreams stopped sprouting once Rosalita was under the earth.

"I can name one," said Arianna, leaning her cheek against Terry's sullied sleeve. "Selena Quintanilla Perez."

"Right," said Terry while dispensing soil into a peat pot.

"Remember Como La Flor?" asked Arianna.

"Yep, even she knew flowers can wither," replied Terry.

"Not in here," said Arianna, glancing around the greenhouse.

"Why don't you concentrate on making something beautiful while you're here?" sighed Terry.

Terry slid a spade towards Arianna. With tentative fingers, Arianna raised her hand to Terry's temple. Terry stopped her before the cloth was off her brow.

"Not my bandanna!" cried Terry.

None of her paper dolls covered their long luminous hair like

Terry in Arianna's homemade design book. The pink and white-striped album contained forty different design ideas from stylish crop tops to tasteful slip dresses. Arianna rifled through the pages searching for a stand-out skirt, so engrossed that she didn't see Ignacio join her in the living room.

In the background, Arianna heard the warm tones of Lydia Mendoza's voice wafting from the den. Ignacio tugged Arianna's lemon-yellow Scrunchie before sitting in his recliner. Her father opened the morning paper which he always read in the evenings.

"You were late today, little lily," remarked Ignacio.

Arianna preferred being called "little lily" instead of "little lady" because they were the main attraction in Rosalita's wedding bouquet. They were also a fixture in Rosalita's hospital room when she was on the ventilator, and a distraction when Arianna didn't want to reflect on the grey smoke damaging her mother's lungs.

"Why?" inquired Ignacio.

"These high school girls on the bus said I could help with their outfits," said Arianna. "They called me their little Selena. I'm going to be a fashionista just like her."

Ignacio adjusted his wire-rim glasses. "You just met these

girls?"

"They're nice students from Domingo High, Papi," said Arianna.

"I wish Terry would go back to school," sighed Ignacio.

The soulful sounds from Lydia's soothing guitar crossed the carpet while Ignacio uncrossed his legs.

"I want Terry to meet these girls," said Ignacio. "Sounds like too big of a job for a fifth grader. I'm not letting anyone take advantage of you."

"But Terry's a drag!" cried Arianna.

"She needs to get out of that greenhouse," said Ignacio while finding the arts section.

"Well, Selena's sister didn't need to be around when she was using her glue gun," muttered Arianna to herself.

"Selena also trusted her family," spoke up Ignacio. "I think that matters more."

It was amusing for Arianna to picture Terry twirling a pair

of drumsticks like Selena's sister Suzette Quintanilla. However, she suspected Terry would board the bus wearing her boring brown greenhouse uniform and read a book on child psychology the entire way. Maybe if she was preoccupied with the text, the trip wouldn't be totally terrible.

"Fine, Papi," said Arianna.

She thought her answer might elicit a more positive response but Ignacio's frown above the paper was deep. Arianna looked over his shoulder to view a memorial article, accompanied by a photograph of a gold-skinned woman in a shimmery purple jumpsuit. The woman's sparkles and seams were impeccable but it's not what Arianna noticed in the year-old concert picture. Arianna observed the elegant sway in her back, the joyous wrinkle of her nose, and her determined grip on the microphone. It wasn't just about her talent or the wonderful threads she wore onstage; it was obvious Selena loved the life she was given.

"At least all the Reyeses have great taste in music," said Arianna.

"Yes, my lily," said Ignacio. "Yes."

Arianna took her father's arm when he presented it to her and they danced to the slow rhythms of Mendoza's rich cadence. Lydia Mendoza sang of their culture's most cherished stories, tales of gold miners and heartbreak that Arianna never wanted to end. The two nonprofessional dancers, one with a loosened Scrunchie, failed to stop until the moon was out and as clear as a Swarovski crystal.

After Arianna misplaced her bus pass, it annoyed Terry, but the reveal of the BeDazzler riled up her chaperone much more. Terry smacked her Juicy Fruit and dug for additional quarters in her polyester uniform shirt.

"Nobody Bedazzles on a bus," groaned Terry.

"Mom did," said Arianna, which was the only defense she could muster.

"This whole thing's crazy," muttered Terry, glancing away with damp eyes.

Arianna remembered that "crazy" was the adjective Terry attached to the day of the fire as well. The police not being able to figure out the cause of the blaze made them all "crazy." Rosalita running into the fiery greenhouse for the cash box was "crazy", even if the girls' tuition was tucked inside. The doctors' inability to revive Rosalita after some promising signs seemed "crazy" to the three people she left behind. Arianna thought flying in to retrieve Rosalita's prize possession was sane in the moment because the BeDazzler made her mother happy. She saw it as a possible consolation, not craziness.

"Please don't embarrass me," moaned Arianna.

"You're wearing jelly sandals with Hello Kitty stickers," said Terry.

"I'll have you know….the girls liked these," said Arianna, folding her arms as the bus pulled in front of them.

The three Tejano princesses were seated in the back with basic black belts on their laps. Yesterday, Arianna offered to stud them with silver gems, and add a couple ruby stones to lead singer Carmelita's belt. She led Terry to the cheerful threesome who was just finishing up the last verse of "Como La Flor."

"This is my sister, Terry," introduced Arianna.

"Hey," said Carmelita. "Can you sew?"

"Okay?" replied Terry, raising her eyebrows. "It's nice to

meet you too."

Terry threw a look at Arianna, and sat two seats behind Carmelita. Arianna rolled her eyes after Terry's comment but kept a grin on her face. She could ignore her sister's saltiness especially after the princesses started salivating over her skirt ideas. Arianna sat next to Inez, the most petite princess, and opened her design book.

"I was thinking black chiffon with well-placed rubies to go with Carmelita's belt," said Arianna, holding up her sketch.

The princesses paused their Discmans. Carmelita played with her hair, tilting her head to one side.

"Maybe you could do the belts first?" said Carmelita. "Then we'll talk?"

Terry shifted in her seat while Arianna clutched her album to her chest.

"A promise is a promise," said Arianna, accepting the first belt Inez handed to her.

Though she removed her psychology book from her purse,

Arianna saw that Terry was simply tapping the cover. Arianna gritted her teeth when Terry chose to tap Carmelita's shoulder instead.

"She's actually really handy with that thing," said Terry. "How much are you going to pay her?"

Carmelita exchanged glances with her friends before staring at her French-tip nails.

"Couldn't this be like a learning experience for her or something?" said Carmelita with a small chuckle. "We're learning too, you know?"

Arianna aimed the BeDazzler's plunger at the leather strap but Terry halted her efforts.
"Terry!" cried Arianna.

"At least look at her designs," said Terry. "It took her hours."

"Ummm, we were thinking about getting the skirts professionally made," admitted Carmelita. "But we'd love to hear your ideas in the future, Arianna!"

The sun filtered into the window but Arianna wouldn't let

it shine on the gemstones she'd brought with her for the belts. She'd already placed them into her pockets after she stood and saw dual looks of guilt in Inez and Patricia's eyes.

"Terry, I don't feel good," said Arianna. "Could we get off at the next stop?"

"Yeah," answered Terry.

The sisters disembarked after the driver pulled up to Dunbar Park. Arianna made a beeline for the nearest bench without acknowledging the fact that Terry was beside her. She deposited herself on the hard wood, trying to imagine why she'd ever thought they were princesses. Was it because they were beautiful and glittery, or so unlike her sister?

"Papi saw this coming, didn't he?" said Arianna. "Terry, they reminded me of…."

"Selena?" said Terry. "No, those girls were lazy. Selena worked hard in everything she did. She was smart and creative…and made her dreams a reality."

Terry released a long sigh before lowering herself to the bench. Pink rose petals from nearby trees swept past Arianna's jelly sandals and Terry's Doc Martens. Arianna stamped on a couple stray petals and dragged them closer to get a better view. Terry's dreams had withered, but they weren't gone. The new Terry may not be the liveliest person or a princess. However, she did share a lot of similarities with the artist they imitated under the covers.

"I bet you could save up for night classes," spoke up Arianna.

"I would like to talk about the books I read," confessed Terry. "And I bet you can make this beautiful."

Terry fumbled with her shirt pocket, removing her bandana.

"Of course I can," argued Arianna. "I'm a hard worker."

"Sometimes," said Terry.

Arianna beamed while applying the faux rubies to Terry's prized accessory. Terry winced when the first stone was set.

"Starting to regret this," groaned Terry.

"*Ay ay ay como me duele*," sang Arianna. "Ay ay ay, how it hurts."

Corazón y Lagrimas

Jim LaVilla-Havelin

Still uncomfortable using Spanish in a poem –
it feels like pretending, even if the words I use
are words I know, words which fit the story…
the story was this:
we came to San Antonio from the North,
from Cleveland and the snow,
came in February 1995
and every day radio on in the car
down Broadway into town
passing Butter-Krust when it still
smelled like bread, and the abandoned brewery
before it became the Pearl
radio on – on stations that played Norteño and
Conjunto – so we could pick up some Spanish.
listened to Intocable and Michael Salgado and of course,
Selena, rising, beloved, already crossing over
passing her salon, which would later become
a CD Exchange. Learned a few words, and heard
a few repeated in so many songs – corazón, lagrimas –
words whose three syllables seemed so much
closer to it than our own, heart and tears.
But we were at the beginning of an adventure,

a new life, so everything was interesting, tasty,
touching, new.
So when the report broke in on the radio
that Selena had been killed (who could forget
John Lennon gunned down in front of the Dakota?)
grief swelled in our hearts, tears in our eyes.
On our way home, passed her salon, where already
in the parking lot an altar was growing, tributes –
candles and flowers, stuffed animals and photographs
weeping fans

> Across days the crowds gathered. The altar and tributes
> grew, the loss and sadness, every time the radio played
> her perfect, present, lively voice. We listened and we
> learned the hard way – corazón y lagrimas.

Love Louder Than a Bom-Bom

Marcy Rae Henry

1.

born the same year

   crecimos singing and dancing to Borderland songs

ni de aquí ni de allá/but not from anywhere else

when *she made it* we said 'she's one of us'

brownproud of hips/lips muy rojos/eyeliner, elongated vowels

and speaking más or menos en español

 con chicana-chic y la nueva cumbia

she helped us seguir adelante

when the media said mexicanos 'were lazy'

  and again/when we were suddenly 'hard workers who would

steal your job' right from under the foreman

just like la frontera crossed us/her music crossed la frontera

   and it lingers on both sides

       ¡chinga la wall!

2.

for the last twenty-five years mi pueblito has hosted a chile-frijole-fest

    just before the leaves start to fall/people come from all over the Southwest to taste the chiles that grow upward/towards the sun

you can smell chile verde roasting in metal tostadores many

blocks
before you reach the plaza/that breaks out in gritos
when the first notes of a Selena song ring out

it's our cue/mami y yo grab hands
and head to the dance floor singing about we're about to do
baila/baila ésta cumbia

    mueve/mueve la cintura
Selena songs never fail to fill the dance floor
i used to think this only happened in the Borderlands
but once i was in a plaza en Perú
surrounded by alpaca stew and guinea pigs roasted red and
brought to the table
with a pepper o un tomate clamped between their long curvy
teeth

    when all of a sudden her voice filled a plaza/that broke out
into a cumbia nearly two decades after Selena nos dijo adiós.

3.

me acuerdo donde estaba when i found out
a kālacakra initiation in Tabo India/June 1996
i'd been living in the Himalayas/sin noticias de mi tierra
believing in Buddhahood/not knowing Selena was gone
the nearer we got to the Tabo temple
the more the altitude sickened between my temples

close to the border of Tibet
someone held my head in her lap
she rubbed my face and asked 'de dónde eres'
i said 'soy de la parte de los estados unidos que era méxico'
'oh' me dijo 'do you like Selena'
'claro/she's one of us'
'did you hear what happened'
it was incredible/the pain in my head spread
to my chest and the pit of my panza
    the stranger asked 'estás bien'
trying to make light (in the multiple maneras Buddhists do)
      cantábamos 'ay ay ay como me duele'

4.

Tabo Monastery was also celebrating its millennium
mil años de mantras and every
day monks worked on a large multicolored sand mandala
    intricate designs where each grain mattered and none stood
out
i hooked my chin over a monk's shoulder/watching in silence
wishing Selena una paz eterna
    on the last day/the monks finished the mandala
and immediately erased the design/like the Christ shooing
his disciple's hands over the bread in Rilke's poem
    all colors of the mandala blended together

así se va la vida/messy and momentary

5.

when i first came to Chicago i didn't know where to live
i visited the Indian barrio y los barrios mexicanos and
after stepping out into the train station in Pilsen/there she was
in chipped colorful paint/next to a mural of la Virgen
Selena
      la mexicana-americana who made it
giving us la posibilidad of making it too

i saw it as a sign and moved to Pilsen
the mural is now gone/(another sign perhaps)
but a larger one was painted in Bridgeport
another in Back of the Yards/otro en el supermercado
cuauhtemoc
    every time i see her face it feels a bit like home
        o me siento más at home en Chicago

6.

the thing is to feel at home in the world
    when we were jovencitas we were told las historias
de Eva/la Llorona/la Malinche
what stories will latinxs of today tell
    a world that hates (some of) them and celebrates

Frida/Lhasa/Dolores/Ocasio-Cortez/Sotomayor/Selena
who will unite us with posibilidades
remind us que

aquí sólo importa nuestro amor

April 16, Spring Birthday

For Selena

Luis Lopez-Maldonado

A spring day boils
alone in my room
the faint smell of *horchata*
lingers in the air,
the wind keeps me up tonight.
Dead orchids hang by their necks:
today the air in the sky can't rise,
spring rain blurs everything around *mí*.
Inside *mí* a sea moves
water spreading like butter
water spreading into sun,
and I trace my brown body
with my index finger.
Today I am lonely:
I touch my brown skin
go in in and listen to birds
sing or scream,
it doesn't really matter.
Outside the trees whisper
and the wind too, and the dead
float somewhere-in-between.

What Selena Means To Me
Christina Ortega Phillips

Music fills my memories. No, music is entangled in my memories; most times the two cannot be separated. And Selena's music is a huge part of my personal soundtrack.

Tú Sólo Tú

I am young and in *la cocina* with *mi abuela* and the air is filled with the scents of *caldo* and the songs of Selena. In between chopping and seasoning, she teaches me how to dance. I loved Selena's cumbias and learned to dance them thanks to my grandma and *Baila Esta Cumbia*, of course, but *mi abuela* always preferred rancheras. Selena had some good ones, but *abuela* liked to listen to her covers.

Amor Prohibido

I am young and I am at home where I cannot fully be myself. *Mi padre* does not like anything of our Mexican heritage and insists that we are American. He tells my mom and *abuela* that I can no longer learn Spanish. *Mi abuela* only knows Spanish. My mom, being raised by parents who immigrated here from Mexico, listens to him because that is our culture. But when I am alone in my room Selena sings to me in private. She, too, did not speak Spanish perfectly. I can relate. I let go of my sadness when I listen to her songs and she fills my head in the forbidden language.

Buenos Amigos

I am Mexican-American. *Mi padre's* words and rules cannot erase that hyphen. Selena's family is from Mexico. I am living in a town where the majority of citizens are minorities. There is a pride in our cultures, our heritages, much like Selena had with her family. On the playground at school my best friend and I sing Selena's songs with pride and no one judges us. My best friend helps me to understand what I am singing.

Entre a Mi Mundo

I am Mexican-American and when I leave my hometown it is not always a good thing. It is a thing that I have to prove, a chore perfectly described in *Selena* when Abraham Quintanilla talks about how exhausting it is to be Mexican-American. But the food, as Selena jokes, gives us strength. As does the music.

Bidi Bidi Bom Bom

When I am sad or happy or want to dance or use the Spanish I am most comfortable with, I turn on Selena and move and sing. The rhythm of her songs is the rhythm of my Mexican-American soul, my pride in my culture. I still get that excited feeling in my tummy *y mi corazon* when her songs come on.

Music fills my memories. Selena's music is part of the soundtrack of *mi vida*, a part of my pride, my cultural connection. *Como la flor* her life was too short, but her impact lives on.

Trascendencia

Seres Jaime Magaña

Aun bajo la luna
Tu canción
En las fiestas
En los muelles
Bajo los faroles
Estos espacios vacíos
Acariciados por tu voz
Estallan, se vuelven estrellas
Renaces
En tu recuerdo sublime
De tu alma son tus flores
Creas
Y sigues creando
Pues la muerte no es la meta de la vida
Aun bajo la luna
Cantan los corazones
Por ti

Songs of Her Life

Juan Manuel Pérez

Just when I was getting so used to you
Just when I was falling in love with you
Just when I couldn't stop dreaming of you
If but once, in this prohibited love
Take my captive heart, wherever you are
A coward with nothing but songs to sing
Left behind with photos and memories
Love me even if the sun never comes
With nothing left, just like that you were gone
Like a flower no more, I come to you
So willing to cry, begging please don't go
With heavy chains, I keep thinking of you
You see that I don't really want to know
Even in the lie, I keep loving you

Selena and I

Maricia Perez Rodriguez

I'll never forget the first time I heard her sing. Laredo, Texas, summer of 1990. A Peter Piper Pizza of all places. "*Carcacha, paso pasito. No nos vayas ha dejar,*" sang the mouse that closely resembled another kid eatery's mouse. I thought to myself, how odd. I had never heard anyone sing about a beat up old car. But the tune was catchy, and I soon found myself swaying to its beat. "That voice," I thought, "what a sweet exquisite voice." That summer and then all through my high school year's, I remember distinctly, hearing Selena and Los Dinos playing over the airwaves in my small, South Texas border town.

When I learned how old she was I couldn't believe it. She was just a few year's older than me! Then I saw her on Johnny Canales' TV show on KIII, the TV station we would pick up from Corpus Christi, and was awe struck. A normal Tejana girl, killing it on the radio and TV! One has this idea of fame and fortune that seems so foreign and so unattainable. Like it's only for the *güeritas*, or for those who live in Hollywood. She became our idol, the Tejanas' Madonna.

1994's "*Amor Prohibo*" album was definitely my favorite and one of her best in my opinion. This also coincided with my senior year in high school, where I felt I was finally started to feel more grown up and more independent. The title track really resonated with me as I too had this impossible love interest. *Como dice la cancion*, "*somos de distintas sociedades.*" Cumbia dancing is my favorite and "Bidi Bidi Bom Bom" was so fun. Around this time, my on and off again boyfriend had moved to an apartment in Laredo. Oddly his apartment was #212, and so in my mind, I connected it so well with "*El Chico del Apartamento 512.*" I just changed the lyrics to #212. The end of my senior year was so bittersweet because even though I was dying to get out of my hometown, I would be leaving behind this guy I had chased for so long. "*Fotos y Recuerdos*" *era todo lo que me iba a quedar de el.* I even wrote him a goodbye letter that I instantly regretted sending.

Selena's ascent continued, and I headed to Texas A&M – College Station. I found my tribe within the dorms at Rudder Hall and the Laredo and Rio Grande Valley Hometown Club parties that played our much loved Tejano music, including of course, Selena. On Friday nights we headed to Bryan, the more Mexican side of Aggieland to go out Tejano dancing. What I thought was just a South Texas thing, Tejano Music, was actually so popular with people from Houston and beyond. Seeing the conglomeration of Mexican American college kids from all corners of the state dancing to her beats really impressed me. My second semester of college, spring of 1995, I heard she would be playing at the Houston Rodeo. Some of my friends wanted to go, being that Houston is not too far away, but then

I thought, "nah, I should be studying. I've got too many tests coming up. I'll just go see her some other time." Little did I know that would be her last concert.

I'll never forget where I was when I heard the news. "Selena has died," announced the Tejano DJ over my car radio as I was heading out to class. It was such a shock. How could a young person that was so much like me be gone so soon? How? Why? What the h***? Thereafter, the Tejano stations played her songs continuously. I came home one weekend shortly thereafter to find that my Mom had bought us copies of her last CD. I could tell that even she was so taken aback by the untimely death.

I was 18 when Selena died. I think I grew up a little bit more afterwards. I had not known any young person who had died. This unfortunate event made me reflect on how precious life is, and that no one is immortal. I drove a little more cautiously, drank a little less, and generally tried to do less risky things.

Her death haunted me for the next few years. Every time I would hear her songs on the radio, I felt joy from the upbeat tunes, but I also felt sadness for the immense talent that was lost. Eventually, I moved on and accepted her passing. I found solace in what her family did to keep her memory alive.

The loss of a loved one is always hard, but the loss of a young person seems so much more painful. Most especially, for a person like Selena, who was a rising star, about to cross-over into the English market to be taken so soon was so deeply painful. I could not even begin to fathom what her family felt.

I met Suzette Quintanilla this past summer at a Latina social event in Houston. Hearing her stories about Selena brought me joy and sadness and suddenly all those memories of my youth came rushing back. I don't think there was a dry eye in the room. I was so happy to have been able to meet such a beautiful soul and hear her stories.

Selena's memory will live forever. In her short time on earth she blazed a trail for so many Latinas living in the US, especially us Tejanas. For that I am forever grateful.

Mi Nombre

Selena Pineda

Hola mi nombre es Selena Alejandra Pineda.
Pero mi familia me llama Sele.
Mi nombre no es solo la combinación de famosas artistas
Selena Quintanilla y Alejandra Guzmán.
Son más que nombres,
La memoria,
La adolescencia de mi mama
Mi nombre traslado por lenguas ajenas la pronuncian
S-e-l-i-n-a
Corrección
Se pronuncia
S-e-l-e-n-a
Cuando era muy chica, al oír mi nombre me tapaba mis dos
orejas
No me encantaba ese nombre que mi mama me puso al nacer
Yo, sonaba tener un nombre gringo o algo mas normal como
      -samantha
      -sandra
      -stephanie
Tenía listas de nombres, pero nunca el mío.
Me tome un largo tiempo de aceptarme/ mi nombre/ yo
Mi nombre tiene poder.

Mi nombre no es solo el tributo de la Reina del Techno pero,
El amor y cariño que mis padres tienen para mi.

S-e-l-i-n-a
Corrección
Se pronuncia
S-e-l-e-n-a

15 in 95'

Santa Ramirez

The police are looking for me, again
It's the second time I run away
She can't hide forever
His tías murmur into their coffee
huddled around the tv set reporting
Selena is dead, Selena is dead
Their eyes are on me
They can't turn me in
or the police will find out
what he did to me
I bob through the sound of the
"Bidi Boms"
but they're blocking the tv
I can't see the news
A voice cuts through the bitter air
of forgotten tortillas
I know she's in there!
my sister yells from
beyond the screen door
I run and hide
From the dark, musky, closet
my ears strain to hear the news

They flip through the channels
but they all report the same thing
Selena is dead, Selena is dead

My trembling hands
pat the blood from my hair
causing it to drip onto my shirt
I stand frozen
I don't want to drip blood
in his grandma's closet
The doors finally creak open
I wince
as light floods in
Ya se fue tu hermana
his wela chirps
as she waves for me to follow
Her pantuflas rustle
quickly through the carpet
back to the tv
The morning bustle has left
It's just me and his wela
Saben quién la mato, I ask
Todavia no,
She bends
placing the now warm steak

back over my swollen eye
I bob trying to see past
her sunny yellow vata
I need to know what happened
to Selena
Arms crossed over her pansa
she retorts
Si estaba enojado
por qué le rezongaste
ya sabes cómo es
My head spins
through the loud
"Bidi Boms"
as the smell of
warm beef and blood
turns my newly pregnant stomach and
spews out my mouth
Bile and blood
a blackeye and a baby
Selena is dead
and mom is gonna kill him

Anything for Selenas

Ruben Reyes Jr.

you spread a bidi bidi bom bom red lipstick over your lips,
the pigment heavy,

     uneven and pushing the boundaries of your upper lip
a bit stains your dark moustache.

slip into the astrodome outfit, one leg at a time,
thighs tightened together when you

     pull the glittering purple fabric over your waistline

como la flor, tanto amor.
you are the flower full of love as you slip the rest of the full
body suit

     over your flat chest
spin in a circle, let the bellbottoms flow

side-step, two-step, salsa, cumbia,
in those shiny silver heels

ignore the aching at the bridge of your foot
ignore when you forget the words and crush your toes

     with a sharp heel

i'm dreaming of you, Selena,
of wearing the bustiers you did.

Poemas Sin Titulo

Minerva Reynosa

1

mamá gritando como siempre gritando en el filo de
los oídos que no la escuchan que no la hacen una
pared de 21 años que se sale con la suya y sí aunque
gritando ella escoge irse casino apodaca 1994
y no hacía mucho que cantaba sus canciones aunque
soy pobre todo esto que te doy vale más que el
dinero porque sí es amor
tal vez era su primera cita o su segunda baby al
contrario sin gritar más que muda mudísima mi
hermana de 21 años se fue para aporranch o apodaca
allá donde vive lupe sí lupe el mismísimo lupe el de
bronco
mamá siempre tiene que hacer un lío
mi hermana se fue con moi a ver a selena y es que
somos pseudo pochos se nos nota el suspenso la
frontera herida abierta aunque nunca tuvimos visa ni
pasaporte ni nada y 12 años después por primera vez
crucé la línea desde la esquina más transitada de
amércia latina otra historia
en ese entonces 1994 en el rodeo de media noche fue
el concierto de selena mi hermana de 21 años con

tanto amor con tanto amor se declaraba
independiente desde la minúscula mitra norte en la
inmensísima ya cuadratura del regio
te mandas sola
y se fue con moi mi hermana de 21 años un poco
fresa de su casa conservadora pero la otra mi otra
hermana la de 20 bidibidibidibombóm la otra la de
20 a ella sí le gustaba andar enseñando su brasier
bordado con lentejuelas como selena
bidibidibidibombóm porque iban a los rodeos a
bailar y salían tarde y llegaban emocionados mis
hermanos todos de 21 20 18
mi hermano por ejemplo dice a modo de leyenda
que guarda una foto con selena en el
estacionamiento del far west rodeo y le empieza a
palpitar así así bidibidibidibombóm
mi hermana llegó esa noche tarde muy madrugada
no pasó nada se hicieron novios ¿? mi corazón se
enloquece cada vez que lo veo pasar y me empieza a
palpitar
pero nunca supimos o nunca supe nada mi memoria
no da para tanto mi hermana no me puede contar
porque estamos lejos y no la localizo
mi hermana en sus 21 años se declaraba desde ese
momento in a *constant state of transit* como dice la

Anzaldúa libre pero desde el acto de salir desde el
centro hacia la periferia aporranch o apodaca como
la nada por el camino ese para llegar al aeropuerto
como la flor con tanto amor de 21 años para
escuchar ver las curvas pochas en traje púrpura de
selena que era la estampa de la chicana empoderada
con tanto amor entre el otro lado y este nuestro
mamá: dice mi hermana
selena dijo: *because i / a mestiza / continually walk
out of one culture / and into another / because i am
in all cultures at the same time*
estoy norteada
bidibidibidibombóm

2

son los 90 y lo que me gusta es el grunge nirvana
pearl jam stone temple pilots soungarden pero
también están tocando por todos lados bandas como
el gran silencio plastilina mosh zurdok movimiento
la flor de lingo el control
era la avanzada regia eran los 90 y en la nave
periódico estudiantil se estaba fraguando la
propuesta 147 anti ranger
no queríamos a los vaqueros a los cumbieros
pantalón wrangler bota roper eran los 90 carlos

salinas de gortari el tratado de libre comercio o nafta
ezln selena y los dinos country jazz polka cumbia
norteña pop rock balada ranchera
es increíble es impresionante que tengas muchas
fans mujeres dice verónica castro en y-vero-américa-
va! porque como mujer a veces es difícil aceptar a
otra mujer o admirar a otra mujer es increíble
es impresionante son los 90 una organización
diferente emergió en el estado de chiapas
profesionales de la violencia nacionales y un grupo
extranjero ajenos a los esfuerzos de la sociedad
chiapaneca asestaron un doloroso golpe a ese estado
y al corazón de todos los mexicanos

3

mi cumpleaños número 16 se marcó
en la memoria familiar por la muerte de selena
iba en la prepa segundo semestre pantalones kriss
kross verde militar botas de casquillo pelo largo
walkman sony y mis amigas me llenaron de regalos
que no recuerdo
crucé la avenida madero tomé el ruta 2 hacia la casa
de mi abuela embarrando tamales mi abuela coco
tenía una modesta tiendita de colonia donde vendía
cocas pan papitas jabones chiquitos y comida a las

trabajadoras de la zona roja de madero esquina con
edison no conocía la palabra teibolera
eran ficheras tatuadas con decenas de piercings
pendiendo de los lóbulos
cuando embarres tamales si te enojas te salen crudos
ni te salen
y salieron los borrachos de carne y frijoles con chile
colorado eran mis 16 y en la t grande de la am a
selena le había disparado
yolanda andrade pariente de sergio andrade
especulaciones
la murieron por no ceder a una transfusión de sangre
testigos idioteces del culto idioteces de los medios
llegaron mis amigos brasileños comimos tostadas
con chile pastel de la lety con coca no hubo festejo
no hubo mañanitas digamos formalmente no hubo
alegría
mi papá llegó a la hora usualmente llegada pero
distinto todos mis hermanos 22 21 19 distintos mi
mamá gritando haciendo un lío el jerez chayo mi
amiga borracha por jerez
se fue el día y se murió selena todas las de cd juárez
todas y fue es un feminicidio y nada de lío de faldas
y fue feminicidio y la mataron y no cantó y la
callaron y nos siguen matando van cayendo

hay una parte en mi que rechaza tomar órdenes de
otras autoridades que rechaza la idea que nos están
muriendo

Selena Cover Band

Iliana Rocha

I sit in a middle school that was once a nightclub. My partner teaches sixth-grade English, & his classroom is on the stage where the quinceañeras used to take place. The room still feels haunted by shuffling tulle. Above the stage, a DJ booth hovers.

We listen to a Selena cover band, & the red school walls are covered in the kids' self-portraits. *Ay, ay, ay, come me duele*, she sings, then into "Amor Prohibido," then a return to "Como la Flor." The singer sounds like more than an echo, as if an echo had a pulse, & I picture Selena running backward into the hotel room, the bullet leaving the wound, returning to its barrel. The gun leaping from the Gulf back onto the Corpus Christi Bridge. The things in this room were never dead, I tell myself.

Like my grandfather. Like the Spanish I never earned, my tongue is wrapped in duct tape, trying too hard to work in the name of instinct. There is a group of boys behind me trying to trick everyone into eating a mouthful of the spiciest salsa while I struggle into a scene of my childhood: I was two, legs dangling out of a stroller. It was in Guanajuato that I first came into consciousness, at the Museo de las Mumias. Pushed between rows of vitrines, I felt my family. I still smelled of the hotel pool, too young to really swim or understand what it meant that these bodies never fully decomposed. Nothing existed before that moment, but I can't be sure I remember it right—the mummies' skin, bones throwing punches inside wrinkled paper bags?

My mother says I was too young, that consciousness comes later, & maybe that's true, & I wonder if, ultimately, she was right in not teaching us Spanish, if her self-hatred has given her the protection in life she needed. The city where she was born, Newgulf, is now deserted because of the rapid drop in sulfur prices in 1956, so we can't even visit. We used to drive by the town hospital before it was demolished, remark about how we were sure it, like my mother, was troubled by more than its broken windows & boarded doors, nails exposed & rusted.

I sing the loudest to the Selena cover band since I still have a lot left to prove as a light-skinned, poorly-Spanish-speaking Chicanx who finds the space between past & present, the rip getting bigger when they play Marc Anthony's "Vivir Mi Vida," & like always, my Mexicanness just out of reach. Those beginnings almost homicidal, threaten to pull a knife on the ineffable I've been given:

güera, you white girl, I can tell you don't really speak Spanish, your
grandma wants to know how you've been eating, I see you have the
body, but you don't have the language, she's all shoulders when she
dances, no hips—

a lifetime's amalgam of a sadness I've had to look up in the
dictionary: *la tristeza.*

Poco a Poquito

Eddie Vega

I could Fall in Love
But I'm stuck Dreaming of You
Missing Selena

It was an '86 Nissan
long-bed pickup truck
white
a little dented in spots
some I made myself
some were made for me
regardless, since the truck was always getting hit
my sister nicknamed it
La Piñata

But the radio worked fine

I'm not sure I ever heard her in the truck though
I played soft rock and country when I drove
Tejano was reserved for backyard barbecues
wedding receptions
quinceañeras

I doubt my high school friends knew that I knew those songs
I tried to escape those songs
They were R.E.M., not Ramon Ayala
Morrisey, not Emilio Navaira

That changed after I
saw her
saw her at the park
saw her at the park in McAllen
My mom said to not get too close
I'm not sure if she was protecting us from the crowd
or what my teenage eyes might see

Selena
all in black
dancing, arms out, con chaca chaca

When she sang
I swear it was to me

La Piñata was La Carcacha
People could make fun of me
but I was inspired
knowing that somewhere out there must be a girl
who cared more about me than my vehicle

Twenty-five years and seven carcachas later
I still have hope

Poco a poquito

Te Canto

Andrea Zelaya

Cómo la flor,
con tanto amor.
A prayer song.
A flower song.
To hold on tight,
and also to let go.
Cómo la flor,
con tanto amor.

Singing Selena,

dancing la cumbia,

while making tamales

para la familia.

Cómo la flor,
con tanto amor.

Y cómo me duele
que no estés aquí.

Pero ayer y hoy,
fotos y recuerdos.

Cómo la flor,
con tanto amor.

Amor vivo,
amor siento.
Te canto poemas, reina,
del corazón.

THE CONTRIBUTORS

José Angel Araguz is a CantoMundo fellow and the author of seven chapbooks as well as the collections *Everything We Think We Hear, Small Fires*, and *Until We Are Level Again*. His poems, prose, and reviews have appeared in *Hunger Mountain, Prairie Schooner, Sugar House Review*, and *The Bind*. He runs the poetry blog The Friday Influence and teaches English and creative writing at Linfield College.

Muskaan Ayesha is a poet and aspiring author with two published poetry chapbooks available. (One under the pen name 'Known As Ash,' titled 'Fire And Ash;' and another titled 'Sidereus: belonging to the stars' under her official name.) She is a South African born writer with a lust for knowledge and has a deep interest in literature from around the world.

Vanessa Caraveo is an award-winning author and published poet who is avidly involved in writing. Over the years, her work has been published in many anthologies and across many organizations. These publications include HWG's, "Out of Many One: Celebrating Diversity" anthology, "Boundless 2018: The Rio Grande Valley International Poetry Festival" anthology, and the Raving Press' "Poets Facing the Wall" anthology, all are available on Amazon. In addition, a few years ago, she had her winning essays published for the IMIA for two consecutive years in a row (2013 and 2014). She also has various fiction, non-fiction, and poems published for diverse organizations and websites. Vanessa has been a volunteer and member of various non-profit groups, and hopes to uplift the lives of others while emphasizing the importance of making a positive difference through her literary work. Vane C <vanec2485@hotmail.com>

Eneida P. Alcalde immigrated to the United States as a child, transplanting her Chilean-Puerto Rican roots into Pennsylvanian soil. Her background fuels her writing, which seeks to ask questions, explore mysteries, and elevate the underrepresented. Eneida's fiction and poetry have appeared in literary outlets such as *The Acentos Review, Stoneboat Literary Journal, As/Us Journal*, and *From Everywhere a Little: A Migration Anthology* from 100 Thousand Poets for Change. Her short story "Duende" was selected as the first-place winning entry for the 2018 *Kaaterskill Basin Literary Journal's* Short Fiction Contest. She is thrilled to be the Associate Fiction Editor for *Oyster River Pages'* Emerging Voices, an initiative which seeks to uplift underrepresented voices in literary fiction. You may learn more about her at www.eneidapatricia.com.

Robin Carstensen's In the Temple of Shining Mercy was awarded an annual first-place award by Iron Horse Literary

Press, and published in 2017. Poems are also published in BorderSenses, Southern Humanities Review, Voices de La Luna, Demeter Press's anthology, Borderlands and Crossroads: Writing the Motherland, and many more. She directs the creative writing program at Texas A&M University-CC where she advises The Windward Review: literary journal of the South Texas Coastal Bend, and is co-founding, senior editor of the Switchgrass Review: literary journal of women's health, history, and transformation.

Beatriz A. Ceja Born and raised in border city Laredo, Texas. Beatriz A. Ceja "Miss B" is a spoken word poet, and Licensed Social Worker. Miss B has worked for years with Laredo's youth. She is part of the Laredo Borderslam board as their youth coordinator. Miss B puts her frustrations of work, love, and loss into her heart-wrenching poetry. She was on final stage at the 2013 and 2016 Texas Grand Slam and is the 2013 Laredo Border Slam Champ. Miss B has performed in various slams and TedxLaredo. She's been in 6 Laredo Border Slam teams and continues to show passion for the art of spoken word.

Timothy Daily-Valdés lives and writes in his hometown of Austin, Texas. He holds an MFA in Creative Writing from Texas State University. He has served on the editorial staffs of several literary journals, including *Front Porch Journal* and

Southwestern American Literature. His work has appeared in *North American Review*, *Assaracus*, *Sybil*, *The Chicon Street Poets Anthology*, and *Texas Books in Review*, among others. "For Selena" first appeared in Issue 3 of *Opossum*, Fall 2017.

Nancy de la Zerda Former educator Nancy de la Zerda earned a Ph.d. in Communication from the University of Texas at Austin in 1977. She writes fiction inspired by stories passed on to her by her parents, a WWII veteran and his loving bride from a tiny village in northern Mexico, as well as from her life experiences as a bilingual nerd since the 1950s, first in a westside barrio and later, in a "middle class" white neighborhood. She has published "The 'It' Girls of La Sembradora," a melodramatic coming of age novel about two adventurous chifladas, young primas, in 1930s Mexico, available on Amazon. It is subtitled, "Bulls, Blood and Brujería." Her short story "Lupita's House," was published in Acentos Review's November 2018 issue. De la Zerda is currently writing a young adukt novel, her recuerdos, and a non-fiction project.

Rubén Degollado was born in Indiana, but is from McAllen, Texas, where the majority of his family has lived for generations. His work has appeared in *Bilingual Review/Revista Bilingüe*, *Beloit Fiction Journal*, *Gulf Coast*, *Hayden's Ferry Review*, *Image*, *Relief*, and the anthologies, *Texas Short Stories*, *Fantasmas* and

Bearing the Mystery. He has been a finalist in *American Short Fiction's* annual contest, *Glimmer Train's* Family Matters Contest, and *Bellingham Review's* Tobias Wolff Award. His debut novel, *Throw*, was published by Slant Books in February 2019.

César L. de León is an educator, activist, and poet-organizer for #PoetsAgainstWalls. His work has appeared in *Queen Mob's Tea House, Pilgrimage, The Acentos Review, La Bloga, Public Pool*, and the anthologies *Pulse/Pulso: In Remembrance of Orlando, Imaniman: Poets Writing in the Anzaldúan Borderlands, Juventud: Growing Up on the Border, Boundless 2013/2014/2015, Twenty: In Memoriam, Lost: Children of the River, Antologia Feipol 2016, Along the River 2: More Voices from the Rio Grande*, and *Texas Weather* among others. He has received awards from the Texas Intercollegiate Press Association and the Columbia Scholastic Press Association. An active participant in the local literary scene, he lives and works in the Rio Grande Valley of Texas and makes a mean mole con arroz.

Magaly Garcia received an MFA in Writing & Publishing from Vermont College of Fine Arts. She has been published in *Along the River III*, University of Texas Rio Grande Valley's *The Gallery* (2013, 2015), VCFA's *Synezoma, Francis House* (2017), *The Chachalaca Review* (2018), and *Boundless 2018: Rio Grande Valley International Poetry Festival*. She lives in south-south Texas, is currently working on a YA hybrid thing, and when not writing she is summoning fantasmas to haunt her cat and cacti.

Aseneth Garza Scott is a Rio Grande Valley native who recently moved to Chattanooga, Tennessee with her son and husband. She was raised in Port Isabel, Texas and attended Port Isabel High School where she first started writing poetry for a school event and club named Beat Night. Since then, Aseneth attended and graduated from Princeton University with a degree in Anthropology and Latin American Studies. It was there she discovered a passion for Latin American literature which has influenced her poetry. She has taught AP World History in Pharr, Texas the past four years and will teach middle school world history in Tennessee. Her poems and those of her former students have been published in *Boundless, an anthology for the Rio Grande Valley International Poetry Festival*. Her latest poem was featured in the Nature of The Valley Art Exhibit at the University of Texas at Rio Grande Valley.

Erika Elisa Garza is originally from the magic town Cd. Mier, Tamaulipas, México. She holds a Master's Degree of Arts in Spanish from UTPA now UTRGV with a thesis focusing in creative writing of short stories. Garza is currently a Spanish Dual Instructor at La Joya Early College High School. She is proud of inspiring her students to become published authors in publications such as Antología de Poesía Joven 2016, *Antología feipol Poetas Jóvenes por la Paz:* Young poets for Peace, Young Poets for the Environment: *Antología Virtual del Primer Concurso de Minificción Bitácora de Vuelos 2016*, From Crayons to Crylons (2014), and *Tierra Firme: Revista Cultural Hispana Vol. 9 No. 1, Vol. 10 No. 1, Vol. 10 No. 2, Vol. 12 No. 1*, etc. with over 100 students published and counting. Garza begin writing poetry in the form a song at the age of 11 inspired by Selena's death. Her poems have been published in the FEIPOL Anthology 2018 Edition. She enjoys being a UIL prose and poetry coach and Sponsor of Sociedad Honaria Hispánica. Furthermore, she is a volunteer actress in "Espíritu Bohemio" theater group in which she promotes Spanish language plays in the Rio Grande Valley.

Michael Gerleman is a teacher in South Texas.

Monique Hayes received her MFA from the University of Maryland College Park. Her work has appeared in Midway Journal, Literary Mama, Poetry Potion, Birmingham Arts Journal, Brio Magazine, among others. She's a VONA Fellow and Callaloo Fellow. <peachykeenwriter@yahoo.com>

Jim LaVilla-Havelin is a poet, educator, and community

arts activist. Poetry Editor for the San Antonio Express-News and the Houston Chronicle, LaVilla-Havelin is the author of five books of poetry, the most recent being *WEST, poems of a place* (Wings Press 2017). His work has appeared in anthologies from Mutabilis Press, Dos Gatos Press, and New Rivers Press' anthology of poems about Bob Dylan. LaVilla-Havelin is the coordinator of National Poetry Month activities in San Antonio, and is the 2019 recipient of City of San Antonio's Distinction in the Arts, Literary Arts recognition. Jim lives in Lytle, Texas with his wife, the artist, Lucia LaVilla-Havelin.

Marcy Rae Henry is a Latina born and raised in Mexican-America/The Borderlands. She is a resister, a performance artist and a mediocre musician with no social media accounts. She studied Buddhism in centers from Bodhi Manda Zen Center in Jemez, New Mexico to Chanmyay Yeiktha in Rangoon, Burma (Myanmar), The November Retreat at Kopan Monastery in Kathmandu, Nepal and El Centro de Meditación de Vilcabamba, Ecuador. In India, where she lived for a couple of years, she received teachings and initiations from His Holiness, The 14th Dalai Lama of Tibet.

Marcy Rae's writing and visual art appears or is forthcoming in *Thimble Literary Magazine, The Wild Word, New Mexico Review, The Acentos Review, Beautiful Losers, Shanghai Literary Review,*

World Haiku Review, Chicago Literati, The Chaffey Review and *Damaged Goods Press/TQ Review: A Journal of Trans & Queer Voices.* One of her pieces is featured on *Litro Lab's* UK Podcast and she reads another's story for *Glittership: an LGBTQ Science Fiction and Fantasy Podcast.* Illinois has been (mostly) good to Henry. She received an Illinois Arts Council Fellowship for *Cumbia Therapy*, her collection of Spanglish stories, and a City of Chicago Community Arts Assistance Grant for *The CTA Chronicles.*

Ms. M. R. Henry is an associate producer of the Damisi Multi film *One Day*, that includes of part of her sci-fi story, 'Application for inclusion in *The 5th Golden Records of Greater American History.*' She is also an Associate Professor of Humanities and Fine Arts at Harold Washington College Chicago.

Luis Lopez-Maldonado is a Xicanx poeta, playwright, dancer, choreographer, and educator. He earned a Bachelor of Arts degree from the University of California Riverside in Creative Writing and Dance. His poetry has been seen in *The American Poetry Review, Foglifter, The Packinghouse Review, Public Pool,* and *Spillway*, among many others. He also earned a Master of Arts degree in Dance from Florida State University, and a Master of Fine Arts degree in Creative Writing from the University of Notre Dame. He is currently a co-founder and editor at *The*

Christina Ortega Phillips was born and raised in northwest Indiana. She is the second generation on her mother's side of the family to be born in America; her grandparents came to the US from Monterrey, Mexico. Her hometown was East Chicago, a city that was full of blended cultures and every year held parades for Mexican Independence Day and to celebrate other cultures represented in the city. She grew up learning both Spanish and English though some of her Spanish skills have been lost, her love of her culture has not wavered. Selena and her music were important to her while growing up. Christina has also written poetry and short stories, some of which have been published and can be found on the Infective Ink website. Her work has also been featured in anthologies such as *Nocturnal Natures: A Zimmel House Publishing Anthology* and *Midnight Oil*, both of which can be found on Amazon. She is currently working on a collection of poetry about growing up in East Chicago.

Seres Jaime Magaña is author of the bilingual play The Tragic Corrido of Romeo and Lupe, presented in the Pharr Community Theatre. His poems and stories have been published in various anthologies, such as Label Me Latin, Voices de la Luna, Boundless Anthology of the Rio Grande Valley, and others.

Seres is also host for Saturday Open Mic at Luna Coffee House where he welcomes poets, musicians, and comedians to present their work. Seres lives in the Rio Grande Valley with his wife and three children.

Juan Manuel Pérez the 2019-2020 Corpus Christi Poet Laureate, is a former migrant field worker of indigenous Mexican decent and the author and editor of many poetry collections including the recent anthology, The Call Of The Chupacabra (2018). The 2017 Pushcart Prize Nominee is also a Desert Storm Veteran and a participant of the 1992 Special Purpose Marine Air Ground Task Force Hurricane Andrew Relief Operation. Juan, a native of La Pryor (Texas) and the only life-time Chupacabra Poet Laureate, has been a Corpus Christi resident since 2013 and teaches History for an area public school. The former 2011-2012 Poet Laureate for the San Antonio Poets Association and award-winning poet is also a member of Corpus Christi's Church Unlimited and spends some weekends feeding the homeless with the TACOS NOT BOMBS volunteers.

Maricia Perez Rodriguez grew up in the small border town of Zapata, TX, where she cultivated a love of music, especially Tejano, art and literature. She studied journalism and briefly worked in both newspaper and television news writing. The environment and the water quality of the Rio Grande River have also been a passion for her, for which she decided to major and graduate with a Bachelor of Science in Environmental Science from Texas A&M University – College Station. She went on to work in environmental consulting as both a field investigator and project manager. She later obtained her Master's in Business Administration from the University of Houston. She later returned to her love of literature and writing while working at Del Alma Publications, an independent book publishing company where she now leads the marketing and design department. She lives in Houston, TX and is a mother of three bright children.

Selena Pineda Daughter of immigrants, Selena is an aspiring writer and artist from Santa Ana, Ca. She writes about her comunidad, her identity and experiences growing up in a produce truck. She enjoys sketching and drawing and exploring libraries.

Santa Ramirez resides in McAllen, Texas. She earned her MA iEnglish with a certificate in Mexican American Studies at UTRGV. She has been performing her poetry in the RGV since 2012.

Ruben Reyes Jr. is the son of two Salvadoran immigrants and an MFA candidate in fiction at the Iowa Writers' Workshop.

His writing has appeared or is forthcoming in The Florida Review Online, Strange Horizons, Horchata Zine, Homology Lit, The Acentos Review, Pidgeonholes, and other publications. He can be found on Twitter @rubenwrites or Instagram @rubenreyes_jr.

Minerva Reynosa (Monterrey, México; 1979.) Poet, cultural promoter and essay-writer. Her books of poetry: *Una infanta necia* (2003), *Emötoma* (2007), *La íntima de las cosas* (2007), *Atardecer en los suburbios* (2011), *Fotogramas de mi corazón conceptual absolutamente ciego* (2012), *Mammut* (videogame, 2015), *Photograms of my conceptual heart absolutely blind*, Stalina Villarreal's traslation (2016), *Mammut* & *Jinba-Itta* (2019) and *Larga oda a la salvación de Osvaldo* with Sergio Ernesto Ríos (2019). Her texts have appeared in journals in and out of Mexico. Her poetry work had been translated into german, english, swedish, russian and french.

Iliana Rocha earned her PhD in English Literature and Creative Writing from Western Michigan University. Her work has been featured in the Best New Poets 2014 anthology, as well as The Nation, Virginia Quarterly Review, RHINO, Blackbird, West Branch, among others. Karankawa, her debut collection, won the 2014 AWP Donald Hall Prize for Poetry and is available through the University of Pittsburgh Press. She is currently an Assistant Professor of Creative Writing at the University of Central Oklahoma and lives with her three chihuahuas Nilla, Beans, and Migo.

Eddie Vega is a poet, spoken word artist, and champion haikuster. His first collection of poems, *Chicharra Chorus* (FlowerSong Books) was published in 2019. Vega is a Pushcart Prize nominee and his poems have appeared on San Antonio windows and on VIA San Antonio buses. He's spending The Quarantine teaching remotely while participating in online open mics and co-hosting the poetry and interview webcast, *Words and Sh*t.* When not in quarantine, find him at a taqueria with a salsa-stained journal.

Andrea Zelaya is a graduate student in her second year of the PhD Literature program at the University of California, San Diego in the Literatures in Spanish section. She received her B.A. in English and Spanish Literature from Texas A&M University-Corpus Christi with minors in Latin American Studies and History, and a TESOL certification. Her current research projects have a literary focus on 20th & 21st century Latin American literature and a theoretical focus on post & decolonial feminism, theories of fragments and temporalities, social space theory, and border theories. More specific research interests include women in Latin American & Caribbean literature,

Central American revolution & postwar fiction, and Chicano/a literature. Outside of her academic research, when she finds the time, she enjoys reading, watching films, writing fiction and poetry both in English and Spanish, painting, learning about diverse things such as languages, architecture, and playing the piano, caring for her plants, taking walks surrounded by trees, and going to the beach.

Book Design

Carlos Galván aka Hawk Beatz 1985-2019, was a shining light in the Bay Area music and cultural community. He moved comfortably amongst many communities here in the US and in Cuba. Loved by everyone who knew him, Hawk was a sweet, loving, soft spoken and spiritual man who was exceptionally talented in music and in graphic arts. He inspired all those who knew and/or followed him. His death December 2, 2019 was totally unexpected and a shock to the Bay Area community who knew and loved him.

Hawk Beatz was a Music Producer of Hip-Hop, R&B, Dancehall & other "New Urban Music". He had much to offer the music world with his unique sound and style. Being from a hybrid of Afro/Latinx & African American culture his approach to music was one of a kind. Born in California and raised both in the Bay Area and Havana, Cuba growing up Hawk studied and listened to a wide variety of music giving him a unique musical ear and understanding of the art form. Music was always a passion and an important part of his life. When Hawk turned 17 years old he relocated from Cuba to the United States to pursue and further his music career as a music producer and DJ. Over the years he also freelanced as a photographer, videographer, and graphic artist. In 2009, Hawk Beatz instrumentals where featured on HBO's "Russell Simmons Presents: Brave New Voices" as scoring for the final episode.

Hawk Beatz produced music for, and or worked with, a number of Bay Area artists such as One Drop Scott, Michael Marshall, Keak Da Sneak, Mistah F.A.B., Kaz Kyzah, Stevie Joe, Ezale, Hunny Tinted, Coco Peila, Nina Davies, Los Rakas, The RapStarz, Thizz, and many more. Hawk also worked with a number of Hip-Hop artists in Cuba and other Latin American countries. He produced music videos and worked extensively on graphic arts for many community organizations. He had his own clothing line through Cubay; produced fliers and websites, for Poets Responding, and Red Earth Productions & Cultural Work; and did book design for Prickly Pear Publishing, CantoHondo/Deep Song Books, and Flower Song Press.

Editor

Odilia Galván Rodríguez – poet, writer, editor, publisher, and social justice activist, is the author of six volumes of poetry, her latest is *The Color of Light*, from FlowerSong Books, 2019. She is a long-time community organizer and volunteer. She has worked as the editor for Matrix Women's News Magazine, Community Mural's Magazine, Tricontinental Magazine in Havana, Cuba and currently edits two journals *Cloud Women's Quarterly* and *Anacua Literary Arts*. Galván Rodríguez facilitates creative writing workshops and offers readings from her books nationally. She is one of the founders of the Facebook page Poets Responding, and co-author of the groundbreaking and award winning anthology Poetry of Resistance: Voices for Social Justice, University of Arizona Press. Her poetry and writings have appeared in numerous anthologies, and literary journals on and offline. She is a practitioner of Indigenous Spiritual and Healing Traditions and strives to live a simple life based on the indigenous worldview of her ancestors